CONTENTS

The 7-Figure Side Hustle	1
Copyright	2
INTRODUCTION	3
Why Delay?	11
Get Rid of Your Fear (It's Doable)	16
How do I overcome my fear?	24
How to Locate a Side Business	34
How to Make Money Using Your Talent	52
28 Side hustles for When You Need Quick Money	63
The Spiritual Imperative: Why You Need to Start a Side Business	114
Why You Should Start a Side Business: The Benefits in Real Life	119
Conclusion: There Are Countless Possibilities.	127

THE 7-FIGURE SIDE HUSTLE

Secrets to Making Money on the Side

Kaitlin Henderson

COPYRIGHT

Kaitlin Henderson @ 2023 Copyright. Without the publisher's prior written consent, no portion of this publication may be duplicated, saved in a retrieval system, or transmitted through any technique, including but not limited to electronic, mechanical, photocopying, recording, or other methods. This book's information is meant to be instructive and enlightening, not a replacement for qualified medical counsel. Regarding any loss or damage caused or alleged to have been caused directly or indirectly by the material in this book, the author and publisher disclaim all duty and obligation to any person or entity."

INTRODUCTION

Are you having trouble making ends meet? I can relate to your suffering.

When was the last time you had enough money to treat yourself, pay off a bill all at once, or just buy lunch for yourself?
It has probably been a while. Why would you need to take up this book if that were not the case?

I got it. You could be prevented from obtaining the things you want and, on occasion, the things you need by life and everything it entails. The moment you refocus, something unexpectedly arises.
Making ends meet and pursuing your goals may be hindered by events like an unanticipated bill, someone's birthday, or payment for the furniture for which you took out a deferred payment plan.
It's understandable why you're having trouble because you don't even remember the last time you were able to save anything.

Imagine this:

Payday has come. Additionally, the week is concluding. There is now a weekend. You have been waiting to get paid to get the landlord off your back for being a week behind on rent. Additionally, you have set aside some money for cocktails on Friday because let's face it, YOU DESERVE IT!
Your pay is sent into your account and presto! All your expenses are covered—at least 80% of your salary. You're left contemplating how you'll use the 20% to see you through to your next paycheck.
Does anything about this situation seem familiar? Or perhaps this

describes you better:

For the previous two years, you've conducted your business from home. Despite earning more than you did at your previous work, you find it difficult to find any extra money to save.

You believe your expenses aren't significantly more than when you were an independent contractor. But for some reason, the moment your money reaches your bank account, it immediately leaves the building.

You struggle to budget your expenses and manage your cash flow because your "payday" is not a fixed day of the week.

If any of these situations strike a bell with you, then YOU KNOW that money, no matter how good you are at budgeting, has a peculiar way of disappearing, frequently faster than you have time to cross things off the budget!

No matter our circumstances, we are guilty of skipping out on necessary expenses in favor of Friday night beverages, fast food, apparel, and everything in between.

We often tell ourselves, "Tomorrow I'll begin a new budget. I'll take a seat and figure this thing out, "only to find ourselves in the same situation come payday.

With these difficulties, it's simple to understand why money and finances, in general, are currently among the most frequently covered subjects in books and articles.

Remember the financial crisis? Some of us are still working to recover from that disaster!

And while there are many publications on this topic, there will never—not ever—be one book or program that solves every problem for every person because we are all individuals with distinctive needs and circumstances.

However, one book offers strategies for your ongoing financial problems that are simple to implement and will have an immediate positive impact on your life.

And what's this? In your hot, small hands, you hold it!

Blueprint for Side Jobs: You can live a better lifestyle by learning how to make an extra $1,000 per month without quitting your day job. This will enable you to purchase the items you desire and pay for them as needed.

It is presented in a clear, simple-to-read manner.

The book is for anyone who has to deal with unpleasant financial consultants who don't care about them, budget nightmares, cash flow problems, a vulgar hatred of credit cards, and a lack of cash flow.

I've perfected the skill of earning money through my "side hustle" as a former full-time worker who did so while maintaining my employment.

After just ten months of daily work, this became my primary source of income.

I researched and experimented with many different concepts throughout this time, which helped me arrive at the lifestyle I currently lead.

I've put together this book to provide YOU the knowledge you need to launch your own side business because I'm very sure you don't have the time (or the interest) to complete all the research and testing I've already done.

You don't have to quit your day job if you don't want to. This book will give you all the knowledge you need to begin going.

Office employees, students, parents, and many others who struggle with money and are looking for ways to make an extra dollar have already found success by putting their plans into practice and acting.

They've read the instructions in this practical how-to manual and followed them.

After reading the first step, Jay, a full-time financial advisor in New York, said he was prepared to start immediately. "Lise gave me so many ideas that it gave me the idea for my own side business, and I read the rest of the book in just two hours so I could start right away!"

Although this book is intended to help you enhance your side hustle skills and earn some extra cash, you will still need to work to achieve these goals. Nothing will change if you don't do as this book advises. It's that easy.

No matter what kind of employment a person has, the concepts and actions laid out in this book offer a guide that anybody, anywhere, can follow. Leigh, an Australian real estate agent in her 50s seeking a means to leave this line of work, is a good example. She started her own side business of freelance writing after reading Side Hustle Blueprint. "I write blog pieces and social media updates for other real estate agents. When I saw the many kinds of side businesses available, it connected with me, and I just put my twist from there."

There is one idea in this article that WILL work for you, regardless of whether you are forced to work in an office, work from home, manage many start-ups, or chase the kids around the House.

As you continue reading, you'll discover the various kinds of side jobs that are available and which ones allow you to get started quickly.
I've been working as a full-time freelance writer and independently published author for the past 2.5 years. I tested many concepts, strategies, and shortcuts to get myself tremendous at this stage.

I had around 10 hours a week that I was willing to devote to my side business when I first began working a full-time job for an employer.

I discovered via trial and error how to generate extra money

without having to quit my day job, which allowed me to buy lunch whenever I wanted and go out for drinks on Fridays without worrying about how I would pay for them.
The actions you must take to start up your side business are divided into sections in this book.

You'll discover:

The several kinds of side jobs you might take up to earn extra cash quickly
Where to get clients because, without them, your side business would vanish into thin air the moment you even consider it
What to put in a proposal when submitting for various side jobs.
According to Richard Branson, the most excellent way to learn anything is by doing.

You'll find straightforward, doable methods to get started in Side Hustle Blueprint: How to make an extra $1,000 per month without leaving your day job. In 30 days or fewer, you'll earn an extra $1000 every month.
I don't go around in circles; the book is to the point. If you continue as you have—struggling and just scraping by—it will help you reach your financial goals considerably more rapidly than if you were to do so.

I also promise that a more balanced financial outlook will enable you to base judgments on what you want and need rather than on a product's price.
Who knows? You might find that you enjoy your side business so much that you decide to quit your job and pursue it full-time!
I'd want to share something with you that you should keep in the back of your mind while reading the book, so please read on before diving in.
You may join the top 10% of successful individuals (think Richard Branson!) by heeding this one piece of advice.

If you don't follow this one principle, you'll develop bad financial living habits than increasing income.
For it, are you prepared? This is it.
Repeat after learning.
You must take action if you want to succeed in life at anything.

Successful people outperform unsuccessful people because they are skilled at learning, doing, and repeating. They swiftly assimilate and put this knowledge to use.
People who think creatively and look beyond their current means of support do so because they are searching for more, in an effort to become financially independent or make changes in their lives that will provide them access to resources they do not now have.

They pick things up more rapidly and put what works right away.

How often do you find yourself saying, "I WISH I made more money. I WISH I had another means to earn money without having to put my work in jeopardy, "only to stop there and never take any additional action to address it?
Avoid becoming the person who sits and says they want to change their financial condition but do nothing about it. Set an example and be the kind of person others go to for advice.
Be the person others see and wonder how they manage to pay their bills AND eat out frequently.
Be the type who acts swiftly to implement what they have learned.

My parting advice is that folks who already have everything they need financially shouldn't keep reading this book.
They have money saved up in the bank, all of their bills are current, and they have the means to buy whatever they want, whenever they want. The rest of us have plenty of room to develop and change. This book is for you if you're unhappy with your financial situation.

Workings Of This Guide

How to Make the Most of This Book

LET'S be clear about something. This book won't provide a quick, simple way to make millions of dollars. It will outline the precise procedures I did to earn some extra money while working a full-time job for you. By following the techniques I'm about to share, I made $1,000 in my first month.
If you want this guide to work for you, the steps must be taken correctly. Jumping ahead means you'll miss out on important information.

It has been demonstrated that the concepts in this book produce life-altering effects. Continue reading to learn how to get the financial resources you need and want.
Each chapter will offer insights as you search for the best concept to help you quickly earn an extra $1000 per month.

Right now, take charge of your finances. Make them work for you so you can live a stress-free existence without worrying about money.
You will find detailed instructions on using this blueprint on the following pages. Then, the crucial step is to choose the appropriate course of action.
Even if you believe you already know something, I advise against moving on. But in the end, I'll leave such decisions up to you because you know yourself best.

This is NOT a comprehensive manual. Finding customers and interacting with them require slightly different strategies for each skill described in this book. But regardless of the expertise you choose to use as your side business, the fundamental ideas remain the same.

This book serves more as an introduction, intended to get you thinking about the various alternatives available and start making some money.

If you're serious about turning your side business into a full-time job, you can learn more about how to achieve that on the resources page at the back of the book, which also provides more information about various skill sets.

WHY DELAY?

Is this the end of it? One morning, while restless at work, I thought. For a Silicon Valley startup that was recently bought by a Fortune 500 business, I served as the sales director in New York. I was perusing Pinterest while on a conference call in my chilly office, which was flooded with artificial light. I looked out the window at the stunning blue sky. Sigh. Then I came across a pin with a line from Mary Oliver's poem "The Summer Day" that grabbed me:

What are your plans for your one wild and beautiful life, please?

My spirit cried out, "Not only this!"

An alteration needed to be made. And so it started. My second job. Does this describe you as well? Perhaps you are stifled in a mind-numbing internal meeting in your air-conditioned boardroom, where the most incredible egos just love to eat up another hour of your life that you can never get back. Maybe you're longing to get to Friday at 5 pm as you wait for your (poor) drip coffee at 8:45 on a Tuesday. Seriously, how does time move so slowly? No matter what.

You can feel a defining moment and know when it occurred.

Many people, like computer pioneer Sean Behr, use their discontent with their day job as motivation to start a side business. Sean describes the period before starting Stratim thus: "I wasn't producing anything new. I've always wanted to start new businesses, new goods, and new ideas as an entrepreneur.

In my case, I felt ready for something else after working in sales for more than ten years, which I loved in large part. I also know that humans are hardwired to seek new experiences and challenges. And I'm not the only one; according to a 2013 Gallup study, only 13% of workers globally are actively engaged in their jobs.

I've read more than 550 books on personal development, and I naturally advise the individuals in my life on finding their purpose, gaining confidence, negotiating, and networking. Naturally, my side business evolved into life coaching.

I enrolled in the coaching school at New York University and used my sales abilities to approach editors with story suggestions. To draw clients, I intended to publish my writing. (There's a reason a hustle is called that!) You might discover that a qualification is not required for the industry you want to enter, so you can start working immediately.

In my case, a steady stream of clients came through my advice-based pieces, and within a few months, I was making money from writing and coaching. I couldn't believe my good fortune! Were you talking to people and giving them life advice for a living? I believe in God. I even had the opportunity to interview some truly unique people while writing for Marie Claire, like Arianna Huffington, Kris Jenner, and Sara Blakely, the founder of Spanx.

I produced several monthly articles and received between $75 and $750 per article (from the publications that paid). I was typing everywhere, including the train, the Whole Foods line, and the office during my lunch break. It took two to three hours to finish each item. Writing for well-known magazines with millions of readers each month provided me with credibility. It increased traffic to my site, which led to more email subscribers who frequently requested my coaching or guidance.

As soon as I started attending classes, I started coaching people for $100 per session. As demand grew (mainly due to people sharing my content on social media) and my life-coaching abilities improved, I raised my fees roughly every three months by $50 increments. I managed my side business while juggling the demands of my day job, which included travel and after-hours client entertainment, and some months I brought in an additional $4,000. In addition to my regular job, I worked 12 to 16 hours per week on it. Based on Nielsen, the typical American aged 35 to 49 watches more than 33 hours of television every week. You calculate with those extra hours each week, what could you accomplish? Consider that for a moment. What improvements in your well-being or achievement of your goals could you make if you gave up or reduced some of your weekly screen time? What would your life be like if you had more money from working those hours?

I cannot express how highly I recommend side hustling. You earn additional income, utilize skills underutilized in your 9 to 5-day job, and protect your investments from a volatile environment. When you launch a business while still working, you can more safely evaluate proof of concept because you can conduct a trial run to see if your side business is viable. This means that before giving something your full-time attention, you can demonstrate that there is a market for it.

However, things aren't always easy. You'll need to combine creative ideas with a strong work ethic to draw in your initial customers and establish your brand. For your hustle to grow, you'll also need to manage cash flow, take care of numerous administrative responsibilities (including outsourcing as needed), and seek methods to make them more effective.

It would help if you were dedicated to this. You'll have to skip your planned Game of Thrones binge session and frequently be the first to leave the bar. You will need to overcome your self-doubt about getting paid for labor, which frequently feels enjoyable. Your new favorite word will be "no." But the reward might be excellent. After almost 18 months of handling my quickly growing side venture, I quit my full-time work. This was no small effort considering that my employment brought in about $500,000 during that last year.

That is how much I valued my new life coaching position and had faith in the growth of my side hustle.
Did folks believe I was crazy? Yes! Heck, I even considered that I might be insane. Long-term, though, it didn't seem all that dangerous. Consider this. The employment market lacks security. I, like everyone else, am subject to termination at any time (based only on one person's judgment!). I weighed the benefits of having control over my schedule, doing work I was passionate about, and losing my wage ceiling (especially as a woman—I felt I'd hit it—against the risk of forgoing a steady job). After all, I got to leave behind an unpredictable boss and the pressure and stress of carrying on with the task that I had grown to detest.

Additionally, I appreciate money and do not take financial risks lightly because I grew up in a home with little money. We were on welfare. Think about whether you are overestimating the risks and whether you can change your viewpoint.

There is a call to action after each chapter to assist you in leaping. To put my discussion's ideals into practice. You could call it homework. As you read this book, I hope these will inspire you. I've also inserted guidance from various fearless business owners and individuals who've launched highly lucrative side businesses. I hope you find them entertaining and gain something from them.

You probably share many similarities with me; all you want is personal independence and ownership over your job. Everybody wants to accomplish a job they enjoy while significantly impacting the world. They are based on our terms. The remainder of this book will motivate you to explore your barriers to success, drive you to go up to the bat and slug it out of the park, and inspire you to take the leap of faith in yourself.

Every hustler out there is not alone. This is a guide on how to embark on your passion project's uncharted territory and seize control of your success.

Next to you

What is the escape route you fantasize about when you're slammed on a conference call, dealing with bureaucracy at work, or feeling overwhelmed by your day job? Make a list of your ideal jobs and a list of your unique abilities. What kind of side business would you prefer? You can begin by posing these queries to yourself!

What issues do I assist others in resolving? What gives me a sense of life?

If money were not a concern, what would I do?

Ask a friend or loved one what you are good at or something you have helped them with if you need assistance. Be receptive to their criticism. If you pay great attention, the answers can simply surprise (and completely thrill) you and show you a brand-new course to take.

GET RID OF YOUR FEAR (IT'S DOABLE)

The general manager wants to see you, Susie. My chest suddenly felt tense. The end is here! I had that thought. I was moving up the ladder!

When I began my career, I was young, naive, and ambitious (not to mention a little cocky). I was desperate to move into sales when I started my first job, which was an entry-level support position. I stayed with the sales team the entire time, listening to them, assisting them with their clients, and upselling wherever I could. "They must be taking notice of this fantastic job!" While completely ignoring the data input I was meant to be performing, I continued thinking to myself reasonably confidently.

I was prepared when the big boss wanted to see me. I put a little lip gloss on and strolled up the steps, ready to accept my promotion in style. Oh, and I was going to ask for business cards as well (in my mind, business cards meant that you had hit the BIG time).

Instead, these words smacked me in the face as soon as my butt touched the chair: "Susie, we're letting you go. It's not going well."

Body-wide shock. My breath came to an end. My stomach dropped. Whaaaaat?!?!

I was in my early 20s, living in Australia, and I had no family to turn to and very little money (they were back in the U.K., where I grew up). However, I discovered a stirring of inner strength through these trying times. When we let it rise, our internal counsel never fails us. It instructed me on what to do. I had to take a risk, stand up, leave, and begin again. Immediately.

I wish I could go back and tell that fearful, depressed girl that everything was OK. Much much better than OK.

Was my anxiety about being 23 years old, living alone in a foreign country with little money—and now being unemployed!—just in my head? No way! I was in fear. There was actual fear. Fear is a genuine emotion. Fear of change is one of the most significant barriers to making any changes in our life.

I'm not here to make terror less accurate. I think I could write 300 books about the topic. Almost every single blog post I've ever published has mentioned it. There are several unpleasant ways that fear shows up. It manifests as justifications. Or I am putting off things. "Oh, I'd love to be a photographer, but I can't make money that way" is an example of how it manifests as practicality. It manifests as uncertainty or ignorance: "I don't know my purpose."

In my experience as a life coach, the most challenging aspect of getting to the heart of a person's desires is getting them to express themselves aloud to themselves, not to me. When we speak it out loud, it gains some strength. Because we are too afraid to express our dreams to ourselves, many of them go unrealized. Dreams become realities when we verbalize them. And given that we are aware of what must be done, this is alarming.

At first glance, it might not seem straightforward, but more often than not, when something worries us, it's because we care about it. It is shedding light on a subject that is so important to us that it COULD frighten us. Because it is capable of. One of my pals, who has a beautiful voice, secretly wants to be a singer. She dismisses it, though, and doesn't reveal the reality of this long-forgotten dream until after a few sauvignon blancs. Why? She doesn't want to find out because she is terrified of what she will have to do. What if she declares loudly, "I'm a singer. I'd like to sing. I would like people to hear me. She finds it much simpler to act as though it doesn't exist. Because what would happen if she made it true by speaking it?

But we can no longer be at its whim once we comprehend fear. So, let's get the lowdown on fear.
The authors of What Happy People Know, Dan Baker, Ph.D., and Cameron Stauth, claim that all phobias fall into one of two categories unless they serve as a protective force that prevents you from doing something risky (such as taking a trip with a stranger, for example). It's only two groups, yes!

A belief in any of the following can be linked to all fears:
1. I AM INSUFFICIENT
2. I DO NOT HAVE SUFFICIENT

Humans have not adapted to account for our brand-new contemporary circumstances. These worries were genuine in the days of the caveman, and if they came true, it meant definite death. The tribe would leave you behind if you weren't strong, healthy, and fit to live. And if you didn't have enough, that is, if you didn't have the resources to provide you with food each day, shelter, and warmth, you would perish.

And now?

In today's society, being "enough" entails having a good education, being well-connected, charming, intelligent, good-looking, skinny, engaging, etc. The list is infinite, especially if you constantly compare yourself to others.

In our society, having "enough" implies owning the things promoted as indicators of success but can also serve as snares: a big home, a fancy automobile, and a great wardrobe. To keep up with our friends, we have to spend money we might not even have on things we don't need.

Despite the vast differences in the situations, the two "reptilian brain" anxieties persist. You can place every fear in one of these categories based on how intense or subtle it is in your life.

I AM NOT ENOUGH is exemplified by all of the following:
I can't tell that person I like them because I doubt that they will find me attractive!

"At work, I'm not allowed to request extra money. It's not like I do my job perfectly.

"Who am I to launch a Company?"

I can't create a blog since nobody is interested in what I say.

"I'm not going to that Party. I have a poor rapport with strangers. Sounds recognizable?

Which of these?

"It's difficult to find the money."

"John has a more excellent family background than I have. I feel a little awkward introducing him to my parents.

"Better to continue with the career I know than to risk failure by pursuing what I truly want to accomplish."

"Tom usually has beautiful things and makes much more money than I do. I believe he is superior to me.
I won't get those boots, that laptop, or a gym membership because I wouldn't say I like spending money.

I DO NOT HAVE ENOUGH, is demonstrated by each of them.

Not everyone will experience terror in all of these scenarios. Maybe you are less of a Party animal and more of an introvert. Perhaps saving up for a trip or a deposit on an apartment is more important to you than going shopping. However, only YOU know your genuine intentions when you speak or think. If there is a justification in your soul for not acting in a fair and ethical way, that's fantastic. If not, fear has you wrapped around its tiny finger, my friend—if your choices make you feel uneasy, unimportant, or unhappy. Fear keeps my friend, a singer, unsatisfied rather than empowered. She stays put to avoid feeling exposed and vulnerable and being forced to perform some job. Using a natural gift for real work with the potential to provide absolute joy. But as my buddy and bestselling author James Altucher puts it, "The largest obstacle we confront to choosing ourselves is rejection and the fear of rejection." Like many of us, my singing friend won't even attempt to achieve that rejection (or its opposite, success).

This can sometimes manifest as doing things incorrectly, driven by external opinions and "shoulds" that place a premium on receiving favor from others. My customer Aaron Clausen, the CEO of the software NatureMapr, has some wisdom on this from his own mistakes:
"Trying to develop or design a business based on where I thought there was an evident gap and opportunity in the market was another lesson I learned the hard way. But I discovered that no one gave a damn about what I was doing. Finding any support or interest was quite difficult. Breaking news In actuality, I was misbehaving. I had established that Company to "strive to succeed." The hardest I've ever worked in my life; it took four

years, and I was only lucky to be able to escape by handing it off to a much bigger fish in the pond. I wouldn't advise using such a strategy. The fun part about NatureMapr is that I simply started mountain biking, bush walking, and exploring outside to escape all my problems, relax, and unwind after I hit rock bottom after much business and job stress. And my next business came to me right there, where I was doing what I loved. It didn't happen on its own; I didn't force it. Please do what you enjoy; don't try to force it.

We frequently avoid this self-examination. All we want is to blend in. We desire the respect and admiration of others. Even when it's not always what we genuinely want, our self-esteem is based on what others value. Even though we are terrified to stand out, what makes us unique and distinctive is what makes us interesting. It makes us attractive, recognizable, and especially valuable to the world. Think of your favorite musician, writer, Actor, or businessperson—anyone who has motivated you. I'll wager everything off your savings that they were considered outcasts or unconventional. Consider Madonna. Alyson Schumer Stephen Jobs Bowie, David. Whatever your opinion of them may be, there is no denying that they stand out. When my friend Alex Cavoulacos, co-founder of the job website The Muse, told me one of her success principles is as straightforward as this: "Be yourself," she tapped into this.

James Altucher, a financial expert, decided that he needed to follow his path. You might be motivated to follow suit by what he told me:

"I was raised to follow social norms from a young age. It's good to stop at stop signs, so you don't damage anyone; it's good to have the education to find a job; it's good to buy a home so you can have roots and create value while your kids have a consistent place to play. These rules were placed in place for good reasons. What is "good" for us has been taught by our parents, teachers, bosses, and even friends. Additionally, trillions of dollars in marketing spend teach us what "healthy" is for us—a $15.00 trillion mortgage market is. The trillion-dollar economy that requires people to feed its engines obediently has a trillion-dollar student loan industry (education is lovely!). It's all good now. However, humans are not standardized objects housed inside a giant robot. In the end, we are unique beings with lives to live. To date, to create our own set of rules that we shall follow. Rules that will lead to our prosperity, happiness, and well-being.

Who will establish our standards for what will make us happy if we don't? The solution is obvious: Everyone else will. Additionally, it is a given that it won't be in our best interests. Not that somebody is actively attempting to harm us. We are the only ones who can decide what is best for us. I frequently had to understand what would be best for me through a lot of trial and error while trying with other people's rules and principles.

What are your rules, then? How do you stop listening to worries and opinions about what you "should" do so that you may act on what you know you must do, regardless of what anybody else thinks?

Next to you

Consider two times when fear has kept you from doing an activity that could have been damaging. What happened as a result? It would help if you were appreciative of your fear of this.

Consider three instances in your life when you were terrified to undertake something you didn't feel prepared to do but mustered the bravery to do it. What were the benefits that each of these three encounters brought about?

Think about a prevalent, considerable worry. Determine whether the concern is one of not having enough or not being enough. Thank your fear for keeping you safe if it is a valid fear—something that may cause severe harm. You can thank fear if it is more likely present just to shield your ego from risk. I'll take over from here.

Think about how you may see your current fear as a chance to develop, learn, and discover more of your inner strength. There is excellent waiting to happen when you sense that stirring within you. Your fear is telling you what to do next. After all, when we reinterpret the experience, it frequently resembles exhilaration. Let's take a moment to acknowledge and honor our fear as an essential component of our growth before discussing strategies for overcoming that fear in the following chapter. Think of five occasions when you were nervous about anything (public speaking, asking for a raise, confronting a friend or relative about something, perhaps) and found that you didn't need to worry as much as you thought.

How did everything turn out? Do you regret doing it?
What does this tell you about your options moving forward?

HOW DO I OVERCOME MY FEAR?

My hands began to sweat. My pulse was pounding. As I gazed into the mirror, I questioned myself, "Why do you constantly do such stupid shit?" I had no intention of scaling a cliff. I also had no intention of breaking the law. I was going to conduct a Marie Claire interview with Spanx entrepreneur and self-made billionaire Sara Blakely.

Marie Claire had long struck me as one of the most excellent magazines (even when I was younger and could never afford it). I'm not a reporter. I did not attend a journalistic program. I didn't even complete my college degree. But after putting a lot of time, effort, and patience into it, I arranged an interview with one of the most successful ladies in the world for one of the most reputable publishing organizations. I was on edge and tense, but I picked up the phone, and the interview took place. One of the world's most innovative executives and I spoke for 42 minutes. How went it?

Beautifully. In her words, I became disoriented. We seemed like longtime friends to me. Sara wasn't just unique, motivating, humorous, and authentic; the essay was widely shared by her staff and posted on the Spanx homepage. To thank me, she even sent me a bottle of champagne.

Similar worries have repeatedly surfaced in me:
When requesting that the discriminatory system for students

who received a free school meal be changed, I went to my school's principal (I was one of them). In front of all the other kids, we were obliged to produce a clear "my family is impoverished" symbol to the lunch lady, which made us feel ashamed.

In my sales profession, I've given presentations to groups of 20 or more in boardrooms in New York and Washington, D.C.

During a live interview on air with a well-known Australian TV program, you talked about asking for what you want.

When I spotted Jake Gyllenhaal in a restaurant in the heart of New York City, I knew I had to say hello (he was lovely).

I knew I had to act like a boss in interviews because I had no network, employment chances, or work authorization when I arrived in New York.

I left my wealthy corporate job at that time. I was determined to work my butt off and had a plan, a lot of faith, and all three. Yet it was still unsettling.

They were tying the knot a second time. I was terrified this time, even though I knew it was correct after my first encounter.

While conducting interviews for Marie Claire, I also spoke with Kris Jenner and Kelly Osbourne. Both of them were remarkably cool and open.

The takeaway? The wheel of your life is in your hands. It's not your fear. Fear will always be with you, no matter how much money you spend on therapy on Park Avenue. However, your worries are not in charge. You do.

The fantastic thing about life and growth is that when you take on new challenges and let your desires, which are more potent than fear, take the lead, your fear lessens. It has no choice but to blend into the background because it has nowhere else to go. Fear fades in the face of action. This I am sure of. However, fear will always be a part of your existence. Not at all. I like to think of it this way: "If I didn't have any fear in my life, would I still be here on earth doing nothing?"

Keep in mind that you once had anxiety before having your first kiss. You were reluctant to travel. Both your first day of work and the first day of school were accompanied by fear. But you continued on your way. The anxiety back then was equivalent to your anxiety today. The problems simply keep getting worse.

The purpose of fear is to keep you safe. Remember that annoying reptile portion of your mind that wants to keep you secure and out of unfamiliar, potentially hazardous situations? Ninety-nine percent of the time, it appears without warning.

Never let your fear take over. It primarily instructs you on what to do next. Recently, my friend Molly shared her two favorite quotes about fear: "Courage is not the absence of fear but rather the determination that something else is more important than fear. It's not fair, but the way things work is that we get the Courage to do the things that scare us shitless after we do them, not before." When expressing how he overcame his anxiety of things not working out, Jason Wachob, CEO of mind body green, said it best for me: "I had launched and been a part of early-stage firms that didn't function, so I knew that it wasn't the end of the world (if I failed). When I was only 19 years old, my Father too passed away abruptly from a heart attack. Even though losing a parent when you're young is painful, you can survive it. Things like failure or rejection don't seem like a big issue when you've gone through that kind of suffering.

Regarding this, too. The phrase "believe in yourself" has become highly overused. This can be challenging at times, especially during frantic periods of self-doubt. So you may flip to "trust in your job" when turning your side business into a reality. You might have had a rough day at work one exhausted Thursday and returned home to a disgruntled side hustle client (this will happen, and it's OK). You'll be depressed, exhausted, and wondering, "Why am I doing this?" You'll be tempted to give up, go to bed, or sit in front of the TV till your eyes are square. But it will pass, and soon you will have a fantastic day at work, a delighted client, and more money in your account than you had anticipated in a month.

In these circumstances, consider if pursuing your dream or letting it end due to a poor day (or string of bad days) is more important to you. Is it developing into the person you were meant to be or holding out for possible never-to-come critique from a foe?

It's time to put it into action.

What will you do today and by the end of the week to overcome obstacles in your side business? Script out that comedy? Purchase the domain name for the food blog you've always wanted to launch. Make a list of email addresses for people you should alert about the start of your matching service, personal branding Company, or life coaching firm.

Go a little bit. Today. Create two deadlines for yourself: one 24-hour time limit.
And a deadline of one week to complete two steps toward the beginning or expanding your side business.

Repeat the phrase:

> *All is well if you have a problem. I am getting the best possible outcome from everything. Only good can come from this scenario, and I am protected. This straightforward affirmation will change your life for the better.*

-Louise Hay, entrepreneur, and motivational speaker

I was depressed before starting my side business as a life coach and writer. Don't get me wrong; I genuinely enjoyed working in sales for a very long time. I excelled at it. Working in advertising is where I made all of my pals. It made it possible for my husband and me to have enjoyable lives. Traveling, meeting new people, and learning about unique and cutting-edge web products gave me the most fun. I felt appreciative of each of those things.

But in that career, I had already learned and perfected everything I needed to. Senior vice president of sales was not something I wanted to be. I didn't want to promote different goods for a different business (as my friend Tal likes to say, "same sh*t, different toilet"). I was prepared to give up what had grown so ingrained in my mind. My gut sensed it. When a shift was not in sight, I sometimes felt pain as my heart raced within my chest. Mark Nepo, a poet and philosopher, gives a great explanation. He claims that "learning, mastery, and abandonment" are three ongoing cycles that makeup life.

I was aware that I had something fresh to master. After half-heartedly offering interview preparation as a side gig, I needed to kick myself in the butt and start a legitimate side business. I looked up a life coach in New York City online and inquired if I could meet her for lunch to learn more about her Company. I used a different coach in the same way. It was great to meet them. They opened my eyes. For them, their work had a lot of meaning. They worked at it full-time too! They had complete freedom over their schedule and volunteered all day. As soon as registration opened, I enrolled at New York University, and my career as a life coach started.

I turned thirty around this time. In coaching, we refer to this age as the point at which we leave "novice adulthood." I felt just that way. It was time to face the facts about my life and the simple job I had to do. I was against an After a decade; I'm still feeling this way (or probably a lot worse). I had put on weight as well. I was imbibing heavily. Because it happened so gradually over time, I was unaware of it. Does any of this seem familiar to you? When you pay attention, there are indications that something has to change. What might you be overlooking? Are you losing interest in exercising (or exercising excessively to compensate for your stress)? Are you declining invites due to tiredness and withdrawal from the outside world (as opposed to declining out of respect for self-care and preserving essential "you time")? Do your friends distinguish between you now, when you were younger, and when you were vibrant and full of life?

I experienced a resurgence of passion for my life once my side business was active, prosperous, and alive. in every case. I had started to kind of like my job again! I considered it to be a stopgap before my "serious career." I saw everyone in a fresh, life-coaching way, including clients, coworkers, and peers. I felt better (and became physically lighter). I began by calling myself a life coach. My coworkers and clients in business were excited for me as well! I did my best to combine the two worlds. It was even said that I looked excellent. It accurately reflected how I was feeling. I was feeling great, so.

For instance, I only became aware that AOL owned The Huffington Post when the Company bought the startup I helped establish for almost four years. Who did I email, then? Judith I. Huffington! What did she then do? She was incredibly kind and complimentary of the writing sample I submitted to her, and she secured my placement as a contributor on their platform by contacting an editor. And who is a regular contributor to their section on healthy lifestyles? Me! That may have even been how you first learned about me. Since then, I have conducted two interviews with her, and she has publicly highlighted some of my work on social media.

Here, we learn two things:

1. You must have creative thinking. Who in your network, down to a few degrees of separation, do you know who could be a valuable resource for you as you embark on your entrepreneurial journey?

2. More influential people are approachable than you think. Because nobody ever approaches them.

Arianna, my "colleague," truly set me up. If you open your eyes and look, there are opportunities around you. Who might serve as a mentor? The side business puts you in that upbeat, energetic, and magnetic frame of mind.

This enormous opportunity would never have been taken advantage of with a pessimistic, restricted mindset. It nearly wasn't, too. For instance, one of my clients in Chicago, after spending a few hours creating art in a borrowed studio, I'm buzzing. She felt restored, refreshed, and alive when she worked on her creative side business. Her energy that day was magnetic —the most lovely side effect of her side gig—and she started a conversation with a stranger at the bar while taking a lunch break at Soho House. The truth is that he had a successful gallery and was also an artist. As "luck" would have it, they ended up becoming close. And as she prepares to make her gallery debut with him, they are suddenly friends with (money) advantages. The truth bomb here is that you get luckier the harder you work (with passion!). This face-to-face would not have happened if she had spent that Saturday morning on Instagram. Instead, things began to fall into place, as they often do once you begin to believe in yourself.

So let's get to the meat of the matter. We must quickly overcome our fear of failing. When talking about starting their Company with co-founder Kathryn Minshew, Alex Cavoulacos of the job website The Muse said, "We were terrified of failure and experienced a lot of rejection, day in and day out—and still do. Thinking through the worst-case scenario helped make it easier: what if we tried our absolute hardest and couldn't make it work, went into debt, moved in with friends or family, and ultimately decided we had to give up on our dream? Painful? Definitely. However, it wasn't something we couldn't overcome. If that happened, we would have to accept the first job that paid us well, settle our obligations, and then determine what to do with our lives. Not what we had in mind, but after considering how awful things may get, we concluded that it was a chance we were prepared to accept. Even if the worst did occur, the story wouldn't be over."

The worst possible outcomes for your side business are presumably those listed below:
Due to startup expenses, you unavoidably lose some money.

You reconsider your proposed side business. When you tell people about it, they laugh. You are unsure of what to do or where to begin. You begin, then stop.
It never generates any revenue for you. Your employer or boss is not helpful.

Your enthusiasm disappoints you. Your side business is terrible. "I told you so," someone says.
The worst-case scenario would be that your side business takes off, you quit your job to devote all of your attention to it, and your new source of income is not financially stable. WHAT THEN? If it happens, you can usually find another work and then do another assessment. This is particularly true if you maintain your network! Nearly nothing in the world of careers is irreversible when you maintain contact with individuals.

The American baseball game offers a terrific lesson in failure and rejection, as my buddy Sean Behr showed me. When hitting a baseball, even the best players in the world fall short 70% of the time. A baseball player who fails does not experience a protracted feeling of failure; instead, they are given another chance to hit in the future. That serves as a fantastic beginning point for entrepreneurs, in my opinion.

What a fantastic viewpoint! Remember that people occasionally lose their jobs and are left without a backup side business. Additionally, if the new endeavor they went for fails, they can leave one job and find another. The more empowered you feel, the more equipped you'll be to face life's inevitable problems and handle them with greater independence. James Altucher's statement regarding freedom and fear is so beautiful: "What I want most is well-being: constantly enhancing my abilities in a passion of my relationships with friends and the ones I love are always getting better.

Always striving to be liberated. When neither worry nor anxiety can drag me down. I am convinced that I can decide what's best for myself and do what has to be done.

Important Information Regarding Impostor Syndrome

Another thing to be on the lookout for when you begin your path to freedom is impostor syndrome. This is one of fear's cunning companions and the fundamental reason why no one ever starts and succeeds in an entrepreneurial endeavor or side business. Be mindful of this pervasive, stealthy drain on your self-assurance Impostor syndrome is what we go through when we feel unworthy of our successes or wonder if we are qualified to launch a business. When we succeed, we can assume we've deceived people into thinking we're capable and attribute our accomplishment to pure chance or perfect timing. We feel like imposters or frauds waiting to be discovered as undeserving of our achievements because we cannot accept our gifts. This explains why many ideally great side businesses never get off the ground. Who am I to... is what we say.

Impostor syndrome, most prevalent in high-achieving women, severely restricts our potential and keeps us from enjoying achievement. We reject fantastic new prospects and innovative ideas because we feel undeserving and fake. Many "what-might-have-been" are lost to impostor syndrome.

That sounds like you, right? I like the justifications I frequently hear (including from myself on my bad days). People I coach frequently state that they are "not ready" for the subsequent action. I am Relocating to a new city, launching a business enterprise, dating online, and submitting a job application to a top employer. In actuality, we are never prepared. However, those that succeed in this world continue anyway. The author Susan Jeffers put it this way: "They sense the fear and do it anyhow." They are aware that they have much to gain rather than nothing to lose by acting. And with time, the more you do it, the easier it gets.

Additionally, it might be pretty exciting. I had never felt more alive when I relocated to a new nation, left my job, and started my businesses. Therefore, keep in mind that it's just an idea in your head and not reality when you hear the voice in your head tell you that you lack the talent or intelligence to achieve your dreams.

Then, turn the fear around and consider: What is the worst that might occur if I start now and believe in my awesomeness? There can only be one way to find out, I suppose.

Next to you

Write down all of your worries. Don't stop there, though. After each one, ask yourself, "And then what?" and what follows? Go on writing. I guarantee you won't end up toothless and living beneath a bridge.

HOW TO LOCATE A SIDE BUSINESS

You'll be working on your side business at odd hours, on the weekends, and whenever you have free time, so you better love it.

The Economy of You, Kimberly Palmer

"Fix significant issues. Solve major difficulties whether you are launching a business or working for an organization. People will want to cooperate with you, purchase your good or service, and probably pay you for it if you can help them with their problem"

Tech entrepreneur Sean Behr

Some of the most prosperous side-giggers I spoke with created ventures that were inexpensive to start, readily scaled as they expanded, worked well with their full-time employment, tapped into their passions and creativity, and, most significantly, were entertaining.

The advantages of a side business have been discussed, and they are innumerable:
- Financial freedom.
- Creative freedom.
- Working on a project that is in line with your hobbies.
- Having more options in case, your day job doesn't work

out.
- The excitement of creating your schedule.

But how can you decide which business concept to pursue?

Countless events can spur you to launch a business. An epiphany, unhappiness at the job, or an unforeseen life event. It was his health, according to my buddy Jason Wachob, author of Wellth: How I Learned to Build a Life, Not a Résumé. "I was operating another firm and attempting to raise financing when I learned I had two extruded discs in my lower back pressing on my sciatic nerve," he said. I could not move and was on the verge of having back surgery. In retrospect, it was most likely brought on by stress and the fact that I was flying approximately 100,000 miles a year, together with an old college basketball injury. Six-foot-seven height and cramped airplane seats didn't help.

My doctor suggested yoga as a potential alternative to surgery. So I started doing yoga every day and was pleasantly delighted to discover that I enjoyed it. I developed an interest in a more holistic way of living. I stopped using harmful household goods and started eating organic. I started my meditation. I've been practicing being grateful. And I fully recovered from my back injury in just a few months (without surgery). For me, it was a true awakening. I saw that health was a combination of how we handle our brains, bodies, and the environment rather than simply being about losing weight or looking nice. Additionally, it served as the impetus for the founding of mind body green.

My friend Rupa Mehta, who founded the New York fitness Company Nalini Method, explains how she got her start: "I was at a crossroads in my twenties, wondering between staying in New York, chasing my adventurous side and passion, or coming back to my cozy birthplace in Virginia. "Teach, teach, teach" kept repeating itself in my ears. It was undoubtedly a dangerous endeavor. Still, I wanted to take a chance knowing I was doing what I truly believed. A studio that clients could refer to as "home" was a need that led to the creation of Nalini Method. I established a business that incorporated my love of home, teaching, and fitness since I realized I couldn't live without teaching.

The secret is to embrace your dreams, no matter what they may be. Other choices are available, including educating and spreading the word about wellness. There has never been a time in history when starting a business was more advantageous. Living in the present is "the opportunity of a lifetime," according to Seth Godin. He is correct. But if you don't seize opportunities, they just sit there.

Here is the tried-and-true method I employ when working with new clients who approach me ready to launch their own side business but unsure where to begin. The formula is known as the Skill Distiller.

The Three-Step Process to Discover Your Talents (That Will Make Money!)
To assist my clients in realizing the strengths they already possess, I developed the Skill Distiller Formula. Just three easy actions will reveal the abilities that will serve as the cornerstone of your side hustle approach.

1. Consider three significant issues you have resolved or achievements you have made.

These need not be relevant to your job. Additionally, they don't have to be exceptional in anyone else's eyes. Just list three accomplishments you're proud of or issues you're pleased to have resolved.

Here are a few illustrations:
In a month, I discovered and paid off my ideal home, coming in $25K under budget.

I supported my best buddy during a very challenging divorce.

I assisted my sister, who was having trouble finding work, in getting a well-paying position that she enjoys.
I placed first in my class when I earned my college degree.
I traveled solo around Europe on a backpacking trip. You can move on to step 2 after you have your list.
2. List the abilities that enabled you to accomplish these three goals.

For a minute, I need you to put yourself aside. This step is particularly challenging for those who are humble or who are dealing with the annoying imposter feeling. You can look at your list and think, "I didn't do anything all that spectacular to obtain those results," if you're used to downplaying your accomplishments.

Though you did, all three of the awesome things you stated above were made possible by a set of qualities and abilities you possess. Nobody else could have accomplished that in the same manner as you did, and not everyone could do it.

Rarely do we stop to appreciate everything we've accomplished and all that we are capable of. But if you want to create a lucrative side business, it's critical to understand your strengths.

Let your thoughts wander over everything you bring to the table that enabled you to make those achievements or come up with those solutions.

Let's continue using the previous example. You reach out to your network to assist your sister in finding employment. You sought to recruit advice from pals who are devoted to their careers. You linked the links between the appropriate relationships to uncover beautiful chances for your sister at outstanding companies.

Your meticulousness went a long way toward improving your sister's resume. For your sister to ace the interview, you helped her portray herself as a benefit to the Company. You also showed her how to follow up in a confident manner that was never intrusive.

Upon reflection, you conclude that you excel in motivating your community to support your objectives. You're fantastic at positioning, you know how to ask the right questions, and you know how to make the most of your relationships. All of these are

If you put these skills to work, they'll create the foundation for a successful side business.
Or, in the event of buying a House, you feel confident conducting the necessary research and sifting through a lot of data to assess the market value of the real estate in your area. You learn that you can keep your composure under pressure and are a decent negotiator due to not letting your feelings cloud your judgment.

3. Consider how you can use your abilities differently.
Doing the best you can with what you have is the key to a successful side business, so keep that in mind. You have a distinct set of abilities that have already demonstrated their ability to produce results. So let's discuss how to utilize them to their fullest potential.

Perhaps you want to start a Sunday knitting class where participants pay you $100 for two hours of instruction.
How can you use your abilities to advance the knitting needle?
Your willingness to ask questions will significantly assist in developing your side business. Who could you consult about forming a weekly group? Who has experience doing this and can help you? Who can identify the unforeseen dangers to watch out for?

You'll also want to rely on your strong network and feeling of community. Can anyone be invited to the club? Who are the influential social butterflies who will immediately spread the word? Who can get your new club featured in Creative Knitters magazine? You had a talent for getting your friends to introduce your sister to their human resources directors. How can you encourage others to spread the news about your knitting group using that same mentality? How can you enthuse individuals to join your neighborhood?

Your persuasive posture and follow-up abilities will be crucial for securing locations. How can you convince the venue that allowing your club to use the space would be in their best interests? How can you ensure you obtain a "yes" by following up in a non-sleazy manner?

Alternatively, you might use your real estate negotiation abilities to gather information, develop, and set the price for a valuable online course that teaches people how to knit, or you could start an international online knitting community.

By examining the current market offerings that other product/service providers are supplying at each price point, you might simply use your natural aptitude for identifying value and price points to your side business.

Your real estate experience has taught you the value of time, so you want to start your online knitting course when interest in the subject increases.

You're not sure knitting sounds like a side business that would be worth pursuing. I know a woman who earns six figures online by instructing knitting. No skill or knowledge is too tiny to be helpful. What talents are you underplaying that others could find admirable and worthwhile to learn?

You'll realize after completing this exercise that you have more than enough abilities to lead you in the right direction.

I had no idea how to pitch editors when I started as a coach and writer. However, I was able to create commercial partnerships from nothing, so I started there and picked up additional abilities along the way.

Right now, you only need to know enough to get started; you don't need to know everything.

Ask someone you love what you are good at as an added step.

Our abilities and capabilities don't always jump out to us since we're accustomed to them. Others, though, see them as plain as day.

If the Skill Distiller Formula is giving you trouble, try telling a friend or a family member what you're good at or what issues you can solve. They'll be able to highlight the inner strengths you possess. Then, consider how you may apply those abilities as you develop your side business.

You'll start to feel highly enthusiastic once you grasp how to utilize your advantages to create the Company you've always wanted.

If you're like most people, you'll experience that feeling of exhilaration, but you'll soon begin to doubt the viability of your plan. Don't! Hold onto your enthusiasm and wait for the concept to develop before attempting to undermine it!

Perhaps some of you won't require this formula. It can be painfully evident that you have a novel inside of you, gorgeous gardens to design and develop in the future, or organic baby clothes to design and produce. But some of us might use some assistance. We are aware of the topics that pique our attention, but we cannot pinpoint our true passion, let alone establish a business based on it.

As I've already mentioned, according to Gallup polling from 2013, only 13% of employees worldwide feel psychologically committed to their jobs. Additionally, according to their 2015 report, millennials are less likely to say they "have the opportunity to do what they do best" at work and many of them are employed in service-related jobs.

Employment that doesn't play to their abilities or talents. This frequently happens because they are afraid that what they actually want to do—whether it is teaching knitting or something else—won't work out. The outcome? Dissatisfaction.

Alarmingly comparable results emerged from my survey of blog readers. Here are the results:
What terrifies you the most when asked?
Not living up to my potential while still on earth, 43.09 percent of you said.

"Not understanding what I am good at and being stuck in my day job," responded 28.73 percent.

Upon being asked, "How would I feel if my employment condition remained unchanged for the next 12 months?"
Not at all; 48.72 percent of you responded.

Okay, I guess, replied 31.66% of respondents.

Only 3.12 percent of you responded with "happy," while 17.7 percent stated, "Pretty excellent. My job is what I desire right now since I adore it.
The feedback was clear:
"Defeated"

"I'm officially bored and stranded," I would require antidepressants.

And last, how much of my existing income (as a team member) would I be ready to give up to become my boss?
19.50% of you indicated that you would give up 30%.
You would give up 20%, according to 23.27 percent.
You would forgo 10%, according to 28.30 percent.
28.93% said they wouldn't give up any of their pay to start their own business.
I recognize this is a pretty loaded topic, and how I phrased it.

It suggests giving up your career entirely. I would not advise doing this unless your hustle is self-sustaining and you have successfully paralleled it with your full-time work.

The answers above are significant because of what they have to say about the current situation. Many people would give up a sizable chunk of their money to follow their passion since they are so dissatisfied with their jobs! If that's not motivation to pursue a side business, I'm not sure what is.

Still fearful? Keep in mind this encouraging information: Your job is not you. Even if you adore your current employment, you are far more significant than what your job title suggests you are and are not constrained by it. As I stated in a piece titled "Your Job Doesn't Define You" that I published for the health and fitness website Greatist. The most common reason clients seek out my life counseling, as stated in my book Here's How To Discover What Does, is that they feel constrained or unfulfilled by their current jobs.

They seek my assistance in discovering their "meaning" or "calling." They are humming along all day at work, seeming to be pleased while feeling irritated. They are drowsy. Their sense of inauthenticity damages their self-esteem. They experience being a "shadow version" of themselves, to use the words of best-selling author Steven Pressfield. They know their ability to do anything but are unsure what it will be. Or where to start.

Unfortunately, nobody is going to deliver you their passion in an envelope, along with directions on how to make it happen. But there are specific crucial inquiries you may make of yourself to figure out what inspires you and calls to you. Being still, turning inward, and being open about what brings you joy—then acting to actualize it—is incredibly powerful. Being in tune with and following your intuition can work magic.

Before you begin using the Skill Distiller Formula, you must decide what your side business might be.
Nine inquiries you can make of yourself are as follows:

1. What do I do when I am not working hard?

Dave is a fantastic engineer and my client. He bought all of the photography gear from an unexpected bonus he received. He spends his weekends capturing pictures of Manhattan and Brooklyn. When he's bored in business meetings or has a quiet hour to kill at the workplace, he reads photography blogs and articles online and follows other photographers on Instagram. He even booked a trip to a European photography exhibition and spent hours at the office researching photography exhibitions. His love for photography was evident to all.

Dave asked me, "Susie, is this what dying and going to paradise feels like?" after a friend hired him to take artistic images for his business website. Um . . . sure! Disclaimer: I do not recommend that you take time off from work, but let's face it, many of us have a lot of downtimes, and what we do with that downtime may be a good indication of what our love for a side business is.

2. What gave me joy when I was a child?

Your interests may vary and develop, but they never really leave you, despite what you might think. What brought you joy when you were young—playing music, writing stories, assisting animals, leading a sports team, or creating things? The Chicken Soup for the Soul series co-author and motivational speaker Jack Canfield suggests performing a "joy review."

Note the moments in your life when you were happiest. Was it when you took an inexpensive backpacking trip through Asia? Lead the high school debate team? Educated interns at the workplace? or furnished your prior two residences? You'll probably notice a theme running across those happy times. It's simpler to make connections when everything is written down.

3. What websites and publications do I adore?

When you turn on your laptop, consider the top five websites you visit. I once worked with a real estate agent who would spend hours browsing cookbooks, websites, and blogs on organic cuisine. He now has a respectable following as a food blogger and generates little income from it. Look at the people you follow on Facebook and Instagram (besides your buddies).

4. If I had unlimited funds, what would I do all day?

Even wealthy people, it's true, need to work to stay motivated (just look at Oprah Winfrey and Richard Branson). For that work, THEY SIMPLY DO WHAT THEY WANT TO DO! That is true freedom. What would you do if you were in my shoes? Would you write, instruct scuba, or offer dating counsel? What activities you enjoy the most and what presumably comes naturally to you are implied by work that you would undertake for free.

5. Who would I choose to be for a week if I could be anyone?

Who we admire greatly influences who we secretly aspire to be. Do you admire Victoria Beckham, Erin Burnett, Matt Lauer, Abby Wambach, or Sophia Amoruso? Review your obsessions—they contain a very clear clue.

6. What gives me the least amount of anxiety?

People are amusing. We are excessively critical of ourselves, eager to point out our mistakes, and reluctant to acknowledge our accomplishments. Getting a very successful CEO I previously coached to discuss her leadership strengths with me wasn't easy.

If this describes you, consider what aspects of yourself you detest the least rather than what you appreciate most about yourself. Permit yourself to reflect on prior successes or instances when you truly assisted people. Allow those aspects of yourself that you may inwardly be proud to shine genuinely.

7. What gives me pure and uncomplicated joy?

Nothing reveals an excellent side business concept like a consistent passion. The main distinction between a hustle and a hobby is that a hustle is financially rewarding and serves a purpose other than personal amusement. Note: If you enjoy painting as a pastime solely for your enjoyment, excellent! That might not be a good business move. However, if you also enjoy painting for others and having your pieces displayed in their residences, workplaces, or beach villas, you might be sitting on a gold mine!

One of my pals loves Krav Maga and teaches it to families; another enjoys throwing get-togethers for her business-minded friends.

Bingo! They may be compensated for their work because they enjoy it, are skilled at it, and excel at it. What do you genuinely enjoy doing that you are excellent at and can be compensated for? Which topic of conversation never gets old to me?
What topic makes you feel like, "I could talk about this all day!" For instance, my husband enjoys discussing real estate investments; he frequently claims that if he had a second career, it would be flipping houses. I find it an absolute snooze fest, but he has a sibling and a few close pals who also enjoy it.

It's crucial to consider what subjects fascinate you and who else can share your enthusiasm for those subjects. It's crucial to cultivate relationships with people you are interested in, which brings us to.

9. What tribe am I from?

People in your tribe understand you. Your coworkers, college friends, or even siblings could not be the culprits. A beloved neighborhood fitness class is where a close former coworker discovered her tribe. She is the happiest and most energized version of herself when I see her around her tribe. It's fantastic!

You can locate a "tribe" if you don't already have one. Utilize all the hints.

Find a group that shares your interests by using the methods mentioned above. Join a reading group. Enroll in a cooking class. At a nearby institution, learn how to code. Volunteer in a refuge for animals. When you glance around and open your eyes, opportunities and people are all around you. At New York University, where I spent my Saturdays learning how to become a certified life coach alongside people of various ages and professions, I made some fantastic tribal friends.

Do you see a more straightforward path now that you've asked yourself these questions? Great! Once you've gained some insight, you must act. Without action, absolutely nothing changes. I was a full-time advertising sales director when I began coaching. I believed my goal was to teach others how to sell. I took pleasure in it, but I soon learned that what I love most is teaching people how to harness their inner strength to feel confident and achieve their aspirations. I know it is possible, especially now that I have made mine real.

What three things can you do over the next seven days to make your passion a reality? Then carry them out. Create that YouTube account and start uploading your instructive videos. Inform your friends and coworkers that you are willing to host a Halloween Party in exchange for a recommendation. Ask the marketing role model if you can buy her a latte in exchange for 20 minutes of her time. There are countless alternatives.

Next week, perform three more. Three more follow. Watch what happens as well. Never stop doing this; keep doing it. You won't believe the outcomes once you begin going.
Keep in mind that tiny, consistent activities have always led to the creation of anything extraordinary. Savings from a few dollars here and there build up to an excellent total. Over time, a healthier body results from wise lunch decisions.

Self-exploration is not an exception to this rule. You can dive deeper inside yourself anytime and awaken your most beautiful, eager, and willing self.

Your job is not you. One aspect of your complex, full-of-potential self is your job. Deep down, you are also aware of it. Why are you holding out? Rumi, a Persian poet who lived in the thirteenth century, said, "What you seek is seeking you." Your bliss, tribe, and delight are eagerly anticipated. They'll be standing by constantly.

Just take some action.

Additionally, in some professions, starting a side business might let your star shine even brighter at work! Aaron, who founded NatureMapr, has a day job in IT. His tool uses crowdsourcing to monitor native species that are in danger. After launching his side business, he learned that having his own product improved his reputation. It truly gives you a small amount of Because you developed the technology Company from scratch and because I work in technology, you also have "street cred" in the industry. In other words, you do what you preach rather than just saying you'll do something someday.

Don't you desire the same improved reputation as someone who accomplishes goals? So start generating ideas today!

Simply identify your passion. Most people have several, but to begin, pick one that satisfies the following requirements: People want/need it, you have a skill for it, and you can make money doing it. It could involve everything from giving calligraphy lessons to organizing parties to working as a freelance website designer. Try not to overthink it. Just start because your business will evolve. What suggestions do you have?

Once more, consider a friend or acquaintance who genuinely supports you. They don't have to be in your life (or alive anymore); they may be your spouse, best friend, Father, ex-manager, or anybody else. It can be a former coach or high school teacher. My Father passed away when I was 19, and I often wonder what he would think of my current job. Consider what this person, who has faith in you, would say about your new Company or creative endeavor. What would they inform you of?

Please listen: They have good faith in you. Your skepticism is unfounded.

Here are a few side businesses you might want to consider:

repurposing homes
Proofreading/editing
home fashion advice, Blogging
, developing organic cleaning and skincare products, etc. Planning events and parties, producing picnic baskets
English second language instruction Driving for Uber, Lyft, or another "sharing economy" app while transporting the elderly health and nutrition coaching
teaching individuals how to prepare taxes more simply
creating logos and other graphic design projects as a freelancer
Wedding or nature photography
Writing wedding speeches.
Catering
financial preparation for fresh graduates from college
obtaining certification as a personal trainer or fitness instructor
publishing steamy/romantic short stories online
Trading options
building bras to order, creating natural candles, Executive coaching for businesses, jewelry creation
Crafts on Etsy for sale
buying for oneself or styling, keeping a YouTube channel active
investing in real estate in markets with solid growth
selling beeswax or honey
making letterpress prints or homemade stationery, working as a referee for a leisure or youth league Social media advice
giving video editing services and assisting customers in creating YouTube videos offering pet grooming or massages for dogs' private instruction
writing grants on the side Licensed massage therapist voice-over work
using a website like Ravelry to create and market knitting designs
arranging people's wardrobes
teaching meditation or yoga

Next to you

List five possible hustling opportunities. Just write; don't overthink. Anything qualifies as one of these, from selling handmade goods on Etsy to selling your famous cheesecake at the neighborhood church. Create at least ten concepts. Although you won't feel prepared for all of them, that's the point. We want to start coming up with ideas since doing so will inspire us to act.

Once you have your ten suggestions, rate each one according to your passion, skill, and the idea's viability. Share your list with a trusted friend who can be an accountability partner and supporter (and vice versa! Ask them: These are my suggestions. How do you feel? What do I excel at here?

Do I have anything missing?

Once you have chosen one from your list, consider the following: Who is already engaging in this? Who might be your partners or competitors?

What platform or format (such as live classes, online learning, physical stores, cookbooks, or consultancy) are they employing to market their goods or services?
What is the breakdown of their prices?
How do they promote and brand their goods or service? How often do they communicate with their client or subscriber base (e.g., weekly or monthly emails with free advice or recipes)?

What CHEAP books or FREE online resources can I utilize to learn more about establishing myself in this industry before investing in training programs or licenses?
How can I distinguish my brand and offering?

You can address many of your initial worries and get a sense of the direction you should be going by responding to the questions above. Consider how your hustle might function within the parameters of these inquiries.

HOW TO MAKE MONEY USING YOUR TALENT

Most of us rarely consider how our passions may bring us money when we think about them. Not all of your passions should be a source of income; for example, you could want to keep doing things for fun, like playing golf, training your dog to perform tricks, writing poetry, or selling old items on eBay. Passion is typically something we do in our free time. Perhaps you enjoy knitting more when there is no deadline to meet, or you adore going to yoga class but don't want the pressure of having to perform the headstand pose in front of others. That's OK. If you are a fantastic cook, you might want to save your skills for the people you care about. You don't have to wish to serve food to guests or impart your culinary knowledge to others. But if you do, consider the number of individuals who would love to learn how to cook or the potential market for your culinary creations. The local caterer was Martha Stewart's first career. Under the name Bethenny Bakes, Bethenny Frankel prepared and delivered her cakes. It would help if you decided which passion you want to turn into a successful business—one that can exist on its own, maintain itself, and that you won't despise as it expands and requires more of your imagination, time, and effort. Then let's get to work!

Being resourceful is the key to success. Utilizing your network is the best method to go about doing this. It is more significant than you anticipate. Please don't hesitate to let your connections know you are available for business, as discussed in the previous chapter. Share your elevator pitch with everyone you encounter, post your side hustle work on social media, and create an email list to keep people updated on your offers. Most people will be on your side. After some time, my corporate clients started to act as coaching clients, and some of my biggest supporters (a few had, or wanted to begin, their hustles).

The following demonstrates how hustles vary from hobbies in that they generate income: When they first started, so many of my coaching and consulting clients worried more about their websites and business cards than they do about finding paying clients, but I was earning thousands of dollars more each month BEFORE I had a website or a business card. Yes, they can be helpful tools, but they can't take the place of your personal hustler's mentality.

Before writing this book, I could have put it off for years as I awaited the results of many interviews. I'll admit that I took a while to publish this (six months behind schedule). But I forced it away.
While looking for coaching clients, I sent the following email to my friends. This might serve as the foundation for your outreach efforts!

Hello, buddies!

I apologize for the mass email.

For those who don't know, I'm now pursuing a Personal Coaching credential at New York University. Now that I have earned my certification, I am prepared to take on some new clients (at a very reasonable charge).

I prefer to coach people I don't know, so I'm asking for your assistance in identifying a potential partner to go on this thrilling adventure with me. It is a six-week, once-per-week engagement (on the phone or in person). Working with people who are determined to bring about positive change in their lives excites me.

I have till 11/18 to give any referrals. I receive a 15-minute call to determine whether we are a good fit. Please get in touch with me as soon as possible if you could send me the names and phone numbers of anyone interested.

Additionally, many of you have already expressed an interest in seeking coaching. If so, kindly provide me with your best method of contact, as I may be able to put you in touch with one of my classmates.

I have a great deal of passion for this industry and know that anyone may succeed in it.

Looking forward to your response. Many thanks — Susie
Start with what you have and where you are. The secret to quickly starting a successful side business is spreading the word, obtaining orders or service requests, and simply START. The idea that you need a lot of money to launch a business is popular. Although I've heard comments like, "Well, you had all this money saved from a lucrative career, so it must have been easy for you to invest it into your firm," my first start-up expenditures were precisely zero dollars, contrary to what many people believe. I made it a requirement of my side business to be profitable, so I had customers before I invested any money in it. I was aware that I would never be able to build my side business to the point where it would enable me to quit my work without taking money out of my savings if it were not self-sustaining.

You do not require a workspace or studio. You can assist someone with their resume in person, on Skype, or even in a coffee shop. People can learn how to housebreak their puppies in parks and apartments. As a self-employed web designer, you can work remotely from any location. With a new customer, my buddy Amber, a photographer and videographer, may earn up to $4K monthly for the price of a cappuccino or lunch. She also gets to decide when and how much extra work she wants. Amber says she frequently takes pauses and will pull back from projects if she feels they are weighing her down too much as she juggles her busy day job with her expanding video business. By never working for free, she also values herself appropriately.

While using this approach can help you get a foot in the door, it's crucial to appreciate what you have to give. Others will do so as well.

Take a look around. Who else could you include on your email list? How may you expand this list? What did you forget to tap? Your volleyball team, please. An ex-coworker? College graduates? Who are the parents of the friends of your kids? Which groups on Facebook and LinkedIn do you belong to? Can your partner lend a hand with their friends? Never forget that the world needs your good or service; therefore, don't be afraid to share it!
Despite being excellent for increasing business exposure, social media is loud and can grow pricey. It's been more brutal (and more expensive) to compete with influencers and companies who have already made a name for themselves due to the constantly changing nature of the numerous algorithms each platform uses and the constantly fluctuating user sentiment.

I get it—having a sizable social media following is attractive, and folks in the influencer marketing industry may make six figures with sponsored tweets, posts, and videos. If you can commit to routinely keeping your social media channels updated, on brand, and helpful to others, it's a terrific environment to play in. Suppose your target market is tech-savvy, and you have unique design or photography abilities. In that case, you might want to put your immediate attention on growing your social media following on Snapchat, Pinterest, or Instagram (#goals). Your best hope will be to use traditional email outreach for less noticeable side businesses.

Interestingly, many marketing professionals in the U.S. think their revenue from email marketing equals that of banner advertisements, websites, and all social media combined! Nearly three times as many people use email on Facebook, and Twitter combined. Have you ever noticed that most social media marketing focuses on email acquisition? Your email address is highly sought after by companies worldwide!

For this reason, creating and maintaining a mailing list is extremely important. You have a compelling method of reaching your audience, regardless of what transpires in the social media ecosystem or which apps appear or disappear. This is not to say that you should stop using social media altogether; it just means that email marketing is still a very effective strategy for your side business.

You can do the following things to expand your list, social media following, and brand:

Invite those already a part of your network (social media, personal email directory). A side note: Unless they sign up themselves, always get consent before adding someone to your list.

Be a guest blogger or presenter for another Company's website, television program, or blog, and include a sign-up link for your website or newsletter. Unless there is a conflict of interest in your offer, most newspapers are OK with this.

On your website, place a sign-up or opt-in page that is highly obvious. Make it extremely obvious since you'll be shocked by how many people who visit and adore your website still choose not to join.

An "opt-in gift" should be made. When they hear this, some people cringe, but It's just an exchange. Did you receive someone's email address? You provide them with something of value right away. The next time you visit a website, pay notice since they almost always ask for your email address and frequently provide you with something in return. This may be a free video tutorial in Krav Maga or a report on the most recent stock market trends.

Grow your subscriber base and prospective sign-ups. Think of every person on your list as a possible customer, business partner, or reference. Use weekly or monthly emails to add tremendous and consistent value before requesting anything in return. Again, most individuals find this problematic.

Even businesses that are not web-based can gain from gaining an online following, but this may not be easy to perceive. Suppose you're a hairdresser, for instance. In that case, you might send out a monthly video tutorial or frequently upload your work to Instagram, showcasing the newest hairstyles or providing instructions on managing a messy bun for a casual date. First, adding value like this makes others remark, "Hey, I like them. I want to support their class, salon, and studio. It is Working with content marketing! It helps others trust and recognize you as an authority on the issue, raising demand for your services.

For instance, this book's original draft was edited by my buddy Hannah. She was a friend of a friend, and as I started to write, she occasionally offered me helpful advice, including tips on coordinating with PR teams to arrange a celebrity interview and having a great opening line. She excels. Our shared passion for reading and writing led to our friendship after meeting at a picnic in Central Park. She is a fantastic freelance editor and writer, and she helped me put this together as one of her side jobs. She even engaged me as a life coach for The Newswomen's Club of New York to organize a vision board event. Over the previous five years, we've employed one another a few times. What is this saying to you? There are people all over. Learn about them. Keep building your network at all times! Both of you will gain from this.

As an illustration, I connected with Stephanie St. Claire, an excellent fellow coach and life strategist, online after reading her writing and tweeting to her. We grew close after she later relocated to New York City! Meeting others who have interests similar to yours is fantastic. I questioned her about the advice she would give someone who wanted to start their own business. Give yourself two years to become completely financially independent, she advised me. Building a base of clients and consumers who respect you, remember you, and are just a little bit infatuated with you is what your first year will be about.

You will serve them in a variety of ways through your writing, videos, free stuff you post with them on social media, and emails you send to their inboxes. You practically have to let go of the cash and keep donating.
"
Everyone is furious over this! They believe they are doing something incorrectly or that their clients are "cheap" and unwilling to purchase their goods. However, all that is taking place is that you are fostering relationships and establishing trust. Sometimes, the balance will tip, and because you have NO CONTROL over when that will happen, simply accept it. But eventually, you'll realize that you're working much less frantically and that the amount of money you're bringing in is double or triple what it was in the beginning. It is worthwhile!

She is accurate. Since they have been reading my free weekly wellness suggestions every Sunday for years, my followers frequently want to counsel me. When you just keep giving, new possibilities just come to you!

The Badass Multiple revenue streams are natural.

When launching their side business, I advise many of my customers to be aware of having various revenue streams, especially in the beginning. Having numerous sources of income is a good insurance policy against the business cycle and fluctuations in customer expectations, just as your hustle is a smart hedge against income unpredictability at work. Also, remember that you never produce your finest work when you need money. When money becomes a concern, you become too stressed to be creative. Your ability to be inventive and choose new chances more carefully will increase as your income increases. That's a critical factor in why side jobs are so alluring. Therefore, diversify to protect your financial reserve!

Having several revenue streams will also enable you to decide what areas you should focus on (from a business perspective) and what areas you should focus on (from an enjoyment standpoint) as your Company expands.
Some sources of income, like online sales of goods, e-books, courses, or rental income from the property portfolio you've been progressively accumulating, may even be passive. You are a source of recommendations for others (and taking a commission from successful introductions as recruiters do).

Here are a few of the ways my Company generates revenue, in no particular order:
Through Google Ads, my blog, personal life counseling,
group instruction, writing for important publications
being a partner in referral for other companies and coaches.

Startups can benefit from Executive coaching, consulting, and advice.

offering my classes online, How to Get a Raise in 30 Days and How to Start a Simple Side Business

These pages!

We serve as a spokesperson for huge enterprises on the subject of trust, Organizing activities like vision board parties.

There is a warning in this. To prevent burnout while working full-time, I just concentrated on #2 and #4. I then included all subsequent income sources. Start with one piece and keep going by adding more!

Before we conclude our discussion of money, I'd want to give James Altucher's perspective on diversifying your sources of income. His belief that the road of accepting a "secure" corporate job, contributing to a 401(k), and working for others for decades until retirement is out of date has enormously impacted my business and life. He suggests something radical:

- You are investing in yourself first, as opposed to the conventional route of relying on historically low raises and salary growth.
- I am conservatively putting savings in a stock plan with high fees.
- They are locking money away in a highly illiquid House with lots of unforeseen maintenance costs.

Unfortunately, salaries have been declining as inflation has been rising, according to Altucher. The average pay for those between 18 and 35 has decreased from $36,000 in 1992 to $33,000 today, and it's only going down. The people I know who are financially the best have several sources of income, do not hold down a single position, and frequently, their work is entirely based on their experience and not their education.

"But what about the arts?" asks education. I got it. The humanities and arts are taught in schools. Additionally, there are many social opportunities at school. However, the truth is that there are a lot of other, more cost-effective, and secure methods to learn these things, given the $1.3 trillion in student loan debt (and rising). Other options would be just as fulfilling, beneficial to your future (perhaps even more so, given that you won't be in debt), and advantageous to society. Every society creates its own "religion" to control the populace. I'm only suggesting, "Don't dismiss that religion." Perhaps many of its principles benefit you, your family, and the people you care about. But always be wary. Make sure you can put your face first in the oxygen mask in case the plane crashes. You can assist most individuals by doing this. Through taking care of oneself. By deciding for yourself.

I had to discard a lot of traditional knowledge to quit my well-paying position with a large Company and devote all of my time to my side business. It's risky, according to conventional wisdom, but sometimes following conventional wisdom is the most dangerous course of action.

Next to you

Accomplish some studies on people performing the work you wish to do worldwide. Look at their websites' "Work With Me" or "Programs and Courses" sections: What emotionally connects with you? They probably have a ton of products available through their Company, including iTunes downloads, books for sale, tickets to events they are organizing, and ways to pay for time spent with them in person.

As a component of their content marketing, yoga instructors might provide retreats, private sessions, and group courses in addition to the odd free outdoor lesson in the summer. There may be additional fees from pet groomers for home visits and various levels of pampering. A one-time wardrobe consultation is one option that stylists have, as is a more involved decluttering of the closet. Pay attention to what excites you and use the concepts to motivate you. Remember that competition in your industry is simply evidence that there is a market, which is fantastic! Use it as inspiration and market research. Which source of revenue do you want to concentrate on developing the most when starting your side business?

Bonus: Work together with other hustlers and business owners whenever possible. Discover your tribe. You will have more "luck" the more significant your community is. What do you know who is now engaged in work compared to what you wish to accomplish? Please list potential contacts and reach out by enhancing their lives! More people will be interested in working with you later if your network is more extensive.

28 SIDE HUSTLES FOR WHEN YOU NEED QUICK MONEY

Happy news The Gig Economy has arrived, bringing a wide range of adaptable alternatives for generating additional revenue. These choices are made possible by cutting-edge technological platforms and the Internet. People of all ages, backgrounds, and conditions can access them.

Remain at home Parents know that raising children can be a full-time job, what with having to prepare them for school, drive them to activities, go food shopping, clean the House, and run errands. Even though being a parent full-time might be tremendously emotionally satisfying, it doesn't pay well.

Similar to how it can be difficult for any household to live on a single or part-time job, it can be challenging to find enough money to cover even basic expenses, much less save. According to a 2015 CNN Money story, you need to make $53,722 per year to live comfortably in Chapel Hill, North Carolina, and almost $67,000 per year just to be a renter in metro Denver, Colorado.
There are methods to make a good living.

Fortunately, it is feasible to make extra money whenever and whenever you want, whether during the day while the kids are in school, at night, or on the weekends. The same opportunities are available if you don't have children but are actively job searching, interviewing, attending skills training classes, or pursuing a degree. The good news is that. The bad news is that doing a part-time job successfully requires a good deal of planning, concentration, and self-discipline. Additionally, you might need to try a few jobs before deciding which one best suits your needs, your family, and your way of life. Additionally, you must be motivated to persevere even on the days when you want to give up or when your peers wonder if you should be working from home. It'll be worthwhile.

The effort will be worthwhile if you can stay the course and remain focused. For the sake of illustration, let's say your annual income is only $10,000 ($200 x 50 weeks). Wouldn't that make a significant difference in your financial situation? You could put away half of it, or $5,000, into an IRA to start saving for retirement if you are currently living on that one paycheck and things are not too tight. And if money is very tight, that $10,000 can help relieve your current financial stress. For instance, it can entail going out to dine several times every month, seeing a few movies, or getting the new athletic shoes you or your children need.

Flexible jobs that won't conflict with your other life priorities
Here are some of the most excellent flexible jobs for earning extra cash on the side or, if you're motivated, to make a full-time salary if you're interested.

1. Earn Money By Testing Websites

Wouldn't you want to know how valuable a website is if you spend hours or even days constructing it? Then you wouldn't be by yourself. Both businesses and individuals regularly solicit input on the usability of their websites. And by doing that, you can make money. What could be better than getting paid to browse the Internet if you enjoy it?

Where internet testers can find work

UserTesting.com is undoubtedly one of the best websites for earning money through user testing. Believe it or not, Google, Wal-Mart, Microsoft, eBay, Yahoo, Airbnb, and Home Depot are just a few of its clientele. This website offers $10 for each 20-minute session that you finish. You'll use websites or apps, carry out a series of tasks, and speak out while giving candid feedback. Your screen will be captured as you use the website or app so that we can keep track of your clicks and mouse movements. Your face won't be recorded, only your voice.

The analysis is another website where you may get paid to conduct user testing. When it has tasks, it emails you about them. You would have to read some instructions for each activity before completing it on the appropriate website and recording your session. A typical job set lasts 10 to 15 minutes and earns $10. The website Enroll will also send you an email when there are tasks for you. The nature of these jobs varies, as does the pay. You might be given a task that takes less than a minute but only pays $.10 as an illustration of this. You would undoubtedly make significantly more money with longer, more challenging work.

The last option is StartUpLift. This business focuses on usability testing for startup enterprises, as you might infer from the name. These businesses give the URLs of their websites, set tasks they want individuals to finish, and then respond with the results. StartUpLift requests feedback, like other websites, and pays $5 for each accepted piece. If you work quickly, you might send up to five reviews daily and get paid $25.

It's critical to realize that StartUpLift only takes submissions when a new startup is published for input, so this is a first-come, first-served situation. As a result, you can anticipate that your submission won't be approved if you arrive late. Your earnings will be sent to your PayPal account weekly if your entries are accepted. Customer service representative is another computer-based job.

To manage voice telephone communications and online live chat requests, many significant organizations in the medical services and other sectors are now hiring customer support professionals to work part-time from home. Ask them if the companies your friends and relatives work for employ off-site customer service representatives.

2. Be A "Looker."

Have you ever considered the possibility of receiving payment simply for going and looking at something? Thanks to the website http://www.wegolook.com, you can.

It has around 15,000 "lookers." Many of them are educators, process servers, veterans in their 60s and 70s, mobile notaries, pastors, and others trying to supplement their income in today's sharing and crowdsourcing economies.

What does it mean?

The operation is relatively straightforward. You fill out an application on the website. You must download the WeGoLook mobile app and pass a background check. When you receive an assignment, you must dress professionally, and when interacting with contacts on-site, you must be amiable and able to execute your "Looks" using a smartphone.

You must be the first person to apply for a job you notice on the app. Website claims, "Typically, you will be given the location of the item or piece of property in question as well as the seller's or owner's phone number, along with instructions on how to reach them. You'll get in touch right away to set up a meeting. You will take a few digital photos there and check off a few basic questions on a checklist. Then, after logging in to your account on our website, submit the photos, and finish the brief report:" You can expect to make between $25 and $200.

What typical "Looks" are there?

You can be asked to record films while seeing a House or flat for a prospective buyer or tenant who lives elsewhere. You can be invited to examine a classic car on eBay or a stylish retro couch that is located 1,000 miles distant from the buyer. You can be requested to investigate a potential date since folks on those dating websites don't always tell the truth. Beyond these instances, you might be requested to look at anything you can think of. Technology enables website visitors to be virtually in two places simultaneously.

Getting paid

WeGoLook offers check, PayPal, and direct deposit payment options. If you prefer a check, there is a $15 processing charge because it must be shipped from Oklahoma. You should have the money in three to four hours if you want to be paid by PayPal. If you want to be paid by check for any reason, it could take up to 10 business days in addition to the three business days required for ACH or direct transfer.

What could you make

Like many of the other jobs discussed in this study, the answer to this issue is that it depends. It will rely on the quantity and pay of assignments you can do. Unfortunately, you do not influence these factors. By simply looking at things and reporting on them, you might potentially earn $125 in a week if you're quick and lucky. You might easily earn several hundred bucks a week with only a few hours of effort if you combine this with one of the other gigs, like testing websites.

3. Discard Outdated Mobile Devices

If you're like most people, you likely have old smartphones or tablets lying around that you might sell to make money. Perhaps you replaced an outdated Blackberry with an Android device, an iPhone, or even an iPad last year. You may find out how much these would be worth on Gazelle's website. You can purchase a certified pre-owned phone on the website if you'd want to save money on a newer phone. What have used cell phones worth?
Not as much as you spent for them, to put it simply. After all, the phone is an older model than those offered now and is likely in use. Here are a few samples of what you might receive in 2015 when shopping for phones on Gazelle: That old, in good-condition blackberry with AT&T as the carrier might be sold for $20. However, a Verizon-owned Blackberry Z30 is worth $75. A G3 VS985 from Verizon is worth $90, whereas the HG Nitro HD P930 from AT&T is only worth $6. Gazelle will pay $100 for an AT&T Samsung Note 3 VS985 in good condition and the same amount for a Verizon Samsung Galaxy Note 3 SM-N900V.

Have a dated tablet?

Additionally, Gazelle buys computers and iPads. In 2015, AT&T customers could get first-generation iPad Airs with 16GB, Wi-Fi, and 4 LTE for $160. A 32GB version of the same iPad will cost $170. Gazelle will spend $30 on a 32GB, 8.9" 4LTE Kindle Fire (keep in mind that these cost far less than iPad Airs) and $10 on an Asus Eee Pad Transformer Prime TF201.

Apple laptops

Gazelle will purchase iMacs, Mac Minis, MacBook Pros, and MacPro PCs from Apple. However, because so many factors are at play, including the size of the hard drive, the quantity of memory, the software update, etc., it is very challenging to provide sample costs for computers. However, it would be worthwhile for you to visit the Gazelle website and see what you might be able to get for your old Apple computer.

Not the only participant

Although there are other players in this market for secondhand iPhones and iPads, Gazelle is a particularly well-known one. Swappa, Usell, and Clark Howard are a few other websites that will buy them, and the latter claims to pay the highest money for your used cell phone.
Consult with your family and friends.
You're not limited to merely selling your outdated smartphones and tablets. Consult your family and friends, as they may still have outdated cell phones collecting dust. They may just give you those old phones to sell if you are particularly close to them—think of your parents. If not, you might have to propose sharing the profit with that friend or relative. Hey, it's still a way to make some additional money.

4. Plan Yard Or Estate Sales

Although estate sales sound better, garage sales are acceptable as well. There is undoubtedly money to be made whether you decide to hold an estate, garage, or yard sale. Naturally, you'll want to sell items that you no longer use. We bet you'll find many items in your garage, cellar, and closets that you either don't need or aren't using. If you have kids, you probably have a ton of toys that they've outgrown. Any tools you don't use anymore? What about the folding tables you purchased for a Party two years ago but never used? Most of the clothing in your wardrobe is undoubtedly outdated and unwearable. Perhaps you have some outdated furniture in a basement corner that you've all but forgotten about.

Are there any books you've already read? Why not include them in the garage sale?

Guidelines for a successful yard sale

You must post an ad for your sale on the local Craigslist. Additionally, you'll want to post signs, but you need to check that there aren't any HOA rules in your area that would prevent you from doing so. According to authorities in the field, your sign only needs to read "Sale" and have an arrow pointing at your home. Post them at significant crossroads close to your home. You might need to put up more signs if your home is far from a major intersection to keep folks in the right direction.
Once your signs are up, have your spouse or partner drive past them to ensure they are visible.

Avoid holding your sale during a weekend with a holiday. The turnout won't be as good as if you choose another weekend. Ensure your lawn is groomed, and no ruts could trip clients if you're holding your sale in your yard or garage. Check the pockets of the clothing you're selling to ensure nothing valuable is left inside. And a rack is the ideal way to show them off.

Make as many of your possessions as appealing as possible, and you might want to move some more intriguing items to the end of your driveway to serve as a type of magnet. Consider having your kids sell iced tea or sodas as an additional income if your sale falls on a hot summer weekend. Stickers should be used to indicate the prices of the majority of your items. Leave the stickers off, though, if there are others where you are willing to haggle over the price. Finally, make an effort to maintain your sale tables' attractiveness by filling in empty spaces as items are sold. You'll require some coins, as well. Few dollars are available for change, but be careful with the money. Some individuals simply have "sticky" fingers.

5. Compose Product Evaluations

Like most individuals, you probably have opinions on a variety of subjects. However, did you realize that you may sell them for money? One reputable review website is called ReviewStream.com.

It's rumored that it's straightforward to earn money writing reviews for Evaluate Stream. You may review almost anything, from diapers to novels, movies (yes, movies) to home goods, and hotels to restaurants. Naturally, you'll need firsthand knowledge of the subject of the review—no copying of other reviews, in other words. You can review your Canon digital SLR if you own one, but not the Nikon DSLR you saw in the store.

If your Review Stream review is accepted and passes the site's requirements, it must be at least 200 words long. You will be paid between $2 and $3 for your review. Even though it may not seem like much, keep in mind that you're just writing 200 words, so it's free money. The site may still purchase your review if it is too brief, the subject is too well-known, or it contains more facts than opinions, but only at what it refers to as its bulk rate, which is its standard charge divided by five. Even though this is far less, depending on how many reviews you can write, it can still mount up. You can tick a box that says you are ready to receive the bulk rate when you submit a review. You can edit your review and submit it again for the total rate if Review Stream states it won't pay you the total rate.

How much may you potentially make using Review Stream?

Would you be able to produce 50 reviews daily or roughly 10,000 words? Would you be able to write five days per week? Writing reviews alone might bring in $125 per day, $625 per week, and

$32,500 per year if all of them were accepted at the going rate of $2.50.

Guidelines for writing acceptable reviews

Your review must express your viewpoint rather than merely a collection of data you plucked from the product's website. This is your chance to voice your opinion if you enjoy doing so. Next, look at the subcategories that are most in demand. You can get information on the Review Stream home page that will be useful by learning the top categories that its readers are most interested in. Third, to make sure the website isn't already overflowing with reviews of the product you're considering reviewing, search for it. Verify that there are no grammatical or spelling issues in your material. Finally, don't get discouraged if some of your initial reviews are for the bulk rate. Simply persevere and keep writing; you will ultimately discover what "sells."

6. Work As A Tutor Or Teach Music Or Sports.

Are you an expert in math, a talented musician, a native speaker of another language, or a math or physics genius? So why not earn money by instructing or educating others using your expertise and skills? Craigslist ads and word-of-mouth are the quickest ways to get started in either of these. Do any of your friends have kids who would benefit from tutoring? Consider visiting the middle school closest to you and speaking with the music instructor there. They might be content to offer details regarding your lessons. Once you get going, you might ask the students about their friends and family. There might be tutoring services in your city that you can sign up for.

You may earn a lot of extra income by tutoring and teaching. A recent college graduate can make between $15 and $20 per hour tutoring other kids, while a high school student who excels in one area can make between $10 and $15 per hour. Advanced degree holders who work as private tutors can make $50 or more per hour.

Working with tutoring businesses like WyzAnt Tutoring, Huntington Learning Center, and Sylvan Learning Centers is another option. Typically, WyzAnt gives its teachers the freedom to determine their fees and then charges a commission for marketing to and paying for the students. The commission starts at 40% but decreases as you spend more time with WyzAnt. Sylvan, in contrast, employs tutors and compensates them on an hourly basis. Tutors employed by Sylvan Learning Centers in 2015 earned an average of $11.72 per hour, according to Glassdoor.com. However, if you worked for Sylvan, you wouldn't need to worry about visiting different kids because you would meet them at a nearby Sylvan facility.

What could you possibly make from teaching music?

This will also vary, but as an illustration, a 30-minute piano instruction often costs between $15 and $40. Just remember that this is an average. Your ability, location, and other variables will determine the exact cost of what you might charge for piano lessons.

The average cost of guitar lessons, which are also very popular, ranges from $20 to $40. For music lessons, one blog recommended $15 to $20, while another message board listed costs ranging from $15 to $65. Finally, according to the Berkeley Parents Network, students should pay between $44 and $55 for music lessons if they travel to their homes and between $35 and $45 if they visit your studio.

7. Perform Mystery Shops

Do you adore shopping? Finally, there is good news. Instead of merely spending money, you may go shopping and earn money.

The trick? To work as a secret shopper, register with Marketforce. You may sign up for free; after that, you'll get paid to eat out or shop for your preferred brands.

How does that function?

As soon as you sign up with Marketforce, you'll receive assignments that need you to visit nearby establishments pretending to be a frequent customer and then report on various elements of your experience. You'll be shopping for some of the top American brands you may already be familiar with. This includes fast food outlets, petrol stations, supermarkets, sit-down eateries, wireless phone service providers, pharmacies, clothing retailers, etc. You'll receive cash in exchange for doing this and possibly reimbursement for any meals or purchases you bought.

What is necessary

Mystery shoppers for Marketforce must be at least 18 years old. You must be highly detail-oriented and have excellent observational skills. Naturally, a computer is required, and high-speed Internet connectivity is advised. A digital camera is also necessary for higher-paying audit-type work.

Become a theater snob.

Additionally, Marketforce provides Certified Field Associates the chance to work as theater checkers (CFA). Here, you would genuinely be compensated for watching your favorite movies. This improves the theaters as destinations for patrons. Every field trip you take as a CFA will be compensated, and you'll even get repaid for your movie tickets and food purchases. You can choose your field visits from various categories, such as advertisement checks, sneak checks, open checks, and so-called blind checks, by playing the field.

How much money can you anticipate making?

Of course, this is another "it depends" situation. It will depend on the quantity and average pay of the assignments you accept. Marketforce assignments pay between $15 and $20, and you may be reimbursed for a portion of the cost if the Company asks you to purchase to receive the entire customer experience. One seasoned mystery shopper claimed to make $14,000 a year from her work. Most likely, you won't make that much money, but if you made three weekly trips at an average cost of $15, you could make $180 a month just by doing what you would be doing.

Additional options for mystery shopping

The chance to work as a mystery shopper is not exclusive to Marketforce. The website Secret Shopper bills itself as the best destination for mystery shopping. Additionally, joining this business is cost-free, and you can pick the time and location.

You desire to shop. Since its founding in 1990, this corporation has been paying between $12 and $25 for every job. A few pay much more. Every month on the 20th, payments are made via check for purchases made the previous month.

8. Pose For Photos

That much is true. Selfies can be sold for money. The website Stylinitity is this Secret. You download the Company's app and register with them. According to the manufacturer, the ideal way to conceptualize its products is as an automated Photo Booth that is placed outside the changing area in retail establishments and features high-quality lighting, a barcode reader, and high-resolution images. You put clothes on, scan the UPC tags of the products you're wearing with the barcode scanner, and then take four excellent selfies of your outfit. The Stylinity marketplace receives these images by auto-upload. Also recommended are your uploads to your preferred social media sites, such as

Facebook, Twitter, Tumblr, Pinterest, Instagram, and others. Your photographs are sent through email and accessible on your Stylinity.com account. Anybody can click on your selfie in the Stylinity marketplace and go to the retailer's official website by following the links to your stuff. If they make a purchase, they receive points you can exchange for money, "exclusive events," or "fun things."

How do you make a living?

You can win incentives when your friends view your images and shop your style on Stylinity. You can receive up to 20% of the sale as a commission if someone purchases, albeit this will depend on the retailer's affiliation with Stylinity. These commissions can be exchanged for money, goods, or other benefits. Additionally, you will receive a $10 bonus right now for joining Stylinity.
Yes, you'd make a great model.

Essentially, you are modeling clothing and getting paid for it. There is no reason why you couldn't make some additional money doing this if you have a good fashion sense and lots of friends. You'll naturally want to be imaginative and put together groups that catch people's attention.
Stylinity is where you can find it.

The business collaborates with over a hundred merchants, including Ann Taylor, Barneys New York, Urban Outfitters, and Nordstrom. Beyond these four, you'll need to search for the Stylinity "Photo Booth" in your usual stores or locate additional merchants who cooperate with Stylinity.

9. Use Your Smartphone To Complete Simple Tasks And Get Paid For Them

Join Gigwalk, use the app, and you might start earning money while strolling through your neighborhood. One of its "walkers" earned $8 simply for taking 20 pictures of various bags of Cheetos on sale at a nearby supermarket to illustrate how much you could make.

What does it mean?

Using a map or a list of gigs close to you, you can apply for gigs after you have a Gigwalk account. To learn more about what has to be done, click on the Gig. If the Gig seems like something you'd be interested in, you can apply for it by clicking the "Apply to this Gig" button. If your application is chosen, you will be notified. If so, you'll select the "Start Working" button "and click to access more detailed information. You'll probably have to download some external applications like Photosynth to do all the chores for a particular gig.

Once the Gig is finished, you submit it using the Gigwalk app. After seeing your work, the client decides whether to accept it or ask a few quick follow-up questions. You will receive payment through your PayPal account as soon as your Gig has been authorized.

How much money can you make using Gigwalk?

First of all, be aware that the pay is typically abysmal. Beyond this, several criteria, such as the total number of Gigs you complete, the distance you must travel, and several other factors, will determine the amount of money you make hourly. Most gigs pay between $5 and $20—nevertheless, some range from $2.50 to $50. Suppose everything goes according to plan; your best chance of making $50 to $60 each day working full-time. Therefore, it is evident that playing gigs won't make you wealthy, but you might make a little additional cash. Furthermore, you might be able to combine these Gigs with Fieldagent (#21), which would significantly increase your income.

Which businesses list gigs?

Consumer brands and retailers typically post these to get firsthand accounts of the circumstances around their goods or events. These businesses typically check to see if things are displayed and priced correctly on store shelves or if marketing events have been executed on schedule and precisely. Most gigs will demand that you submit geo-tagged images as proof of your labor. You require a PayPal account 39 because Gigwalk only uses PayPal for payments. Earn Money Typing or Transcription of Audio

Transcribing legal or other types of recordings could pay up to $15 per hour if you can type quickly and accurately. More than 50,000 people utilize this service globally, including, according to the SpeakWrite website, State governments, law firms, the criminal justice system, insurance companies, and a wide range of business clientele.

What it does

Working at SpeakWrite gives you the freedom to set your schedule, operate independently, and forego the costs associated with regular employment, which is one of the most significant benefits. You can work from home when you choose. When you're prepared to start working, you choose "Click the "At Work" button to indicate that you are available for a task. An audio and visual message will be sent to you when a task is given. After accepting the position, you download the audio and look for additional guidelines or notes. After finishing a task, you upload the files and wait for the following assignment. The SpeakWrite system automatically detects when you are working on a job and won't provide you with any new assignments until you have completed the one you are currently working on.

What must you do to be eligible?

If you are applying for a "generic" typist position, you must have at least 24 months of recent experience in transcription or word processing. You should be proficient in creating official correspondence, reports, and documents. It would help if you had a solid grasp of the English language, punctuation, and spelling, in addition to being adept at using the most recent version of Microsoft Word, including its advanced formatting tools.

You must have at least 24 months of steadily increasing responsibility in law practice and experience setting up legal pleadings, agreements, interrogatories, court headings, disposition summaries, formal communication, and other legal documents. Additionally, you'll need to be proficient in spelling, English grammar, and punctuation. You'll also need to know how to format legal citations. Typists for "legal" and "generic" work are compensated at a rate of 0.5 cents per word typed.

You will require a computer with at least 1 GB of RAM running Windows 7 (no Macs or tablets), a sound card and earbuds, a printer, and a foot pedal to control the playing back of dictated information, depending on whether you choose to be a "general" or "legal" typist. Of course, you'll also need an Internet connection with a capacity at least as high as a DSL connection.

A background check might be necessary since some of SpeakWrite's more significant clients want it. Additionally, the organization has an evaluation procedure that involves a brief activity to verify your typing speed, which must be at least 60 WPM with 90% accuracy. If you pass, SpeakWrite's proprietary typing program will be installed on your computer, and you'll also be given several practice transcribing assignments that you'll be graded on.

What could you make

Your workweek will be planned out in units. How many units you work in a particular week will determine how much you might make. You will be able to take on more shifts if you consistently put in a lot of work for SpeakWrite. Your hourly wage should be between $12 and $15, and some of the Company's typists make more than $15.

10. Trade In Your Old Dvds, Cds, And Video Games

You likely have a ton of outdated CDs, videos, and games stacked up on a shelf in your living or family room. Why not sell your unwanted media using the website Decluttr if you aren't viewing, listening to, or playing it? Its website advertises that it is the simplest method to sell unwanted DVDs, CDs, and games and that using it is free.

After registering with the website, you download an app that converts your smartphone into a barcode scanner. You can get an instant offer for the products you want to sell by scanning the barcodes. If you are satisfied with the offers, simply box up the items and ship them, at no cost, to Decluttr. Once the Company has processed your products, you will be paid by check or direct deposit. It is as simple as scanning, sending money, and spending it.

It's just easier.

Decluttr makes selling your used DVDs, CDs, and games much more accessible than listing them elsewhere, creating descriptions, choosing a price, and covering fees. Additionally, as mentioned above, Decluttr's delivery service offers free shipping on all purchases. You must package up the items you're selling, attach a label from Decluttr, and deliver it to the UPS office closest to you.

How much money can you make?

You won't ever become wealthy by selling used goods, I suppose.

Decluttr's algorithm determines how much it will pay you based on variables, including how many copies of a given title it has in stock, how much the item is going for on Amazon or eBay, and how quickly it sells. Keep in mind that Decluttr doesn't only buy discs. The item must include the disc, a case, and an album booklet or user guide. Additionally, the business's "Goal is to give customers the best deals on DVDs, CDs, Blu-Rays, and video games. For each DVD, you might typically expect to make between $.50 and $1. You might get as much as $3 in some circumstances. You might get paid $0.50 or $2.85 for some CDs. In reality, Decluttr will always pay you at least $.50 for any item you ship to it. Therefore, you would receive $5 and pay nothing for the postage if you sent ten used CDs.

You won't find a list of the prices Decluttr pays for particular things online, so don't look for one. Given that doing so would be against the Company's agreements with Amazon and eBay, this is the only unclear component of its process. Therefore, it's a bit of a crapshoot about how much you'll get paid when you send in those games, CDs, or DVDs. However, this is sort of a "what have you got to lose" situation. Why not give Decluttr a try if you're not already playing those games, watching those movies, or listening to those songs? The future? You might receive a check for $50 or more in a few weeks, which is essentially free money.

11. Make Money Online

Selling products on Amazon, eBay, CaféPress, or Zazzle is simple. You can create your store on Amazon or eBay. It's pretty easy to set up an Amazon store. Even though creating one on eBay is a little more complicated, you can start yours by hiring assistance. For instance, you may pay around $29.99 for a professional Dynamic Shop Package, which includes free installation. Zazzle and CaféPress do not allow you to open storefronts, but you can upload and sell goods there.

Amazon.com

One of the best things about setting up an Amazon store is that you can sell any of the hundreds of thousands of products that Amazon has to offer. But most profitable Amazon sellers specialize in a particular market, such as selling women's handbags, baby apparel, woodworking supplies, or collectible toys. In this approach, potential customers are more likely to see your product when they search for a term like "woodworking tools."

EBay.com

Amazon and eBay have a lot in common. When buyers search for a term, they are presented with hundreds of pages of listings as their results. One feature that sets eBay apart is that occasionally you'll notice a phrase like "We appreciate you selecting XYZ machine. Check my other things as we look forward to making you a delighted customer. You would visit the seller's store if you clicked on that link. Amazon.com, regrettably, does not do this. You won't see a connection to your store when you click on an item on Amazon; instead, you'll get information about the item.

Coffee Press

On this website, you may earn money by making and uploading designs. After that, Café Press will offer your designs on various items, including pillows, phone cases, and coffee mugs. You receive a commission if CaféPress customers enjoy your design and purchase products using it.

Zazzle

Zazzle would be an excellent place to sell your work if you are an artist, graphic designer, or photographer or create or produce personalized or customizable products. You add your products or artwork to make it operate. You can sell artwork that appears on hundreds of Zazzle products if you upload it. Zazzle makes and transports the goods for you once customers purchase them. Your royalty rates, ranging from 5% to 99%, are up to you to decide. To earn money, you must first spend money.

The one drawback of selling items online is that you must publicize them. Without some encouragement, people won't just wander into your business, whether you sell goods on Zazzle or have an Amazon store. The four-line ads in the right column of a Google search are known as Adwords, and you will need to be ready to spend money mining them. Because AdWords is purchased through an auction system, the more well-known the keyword you wish to purchase, the more it will cost you.

12. Work As A Field Agent Or Gig-Walk

No, this situation is not similar to working for the CIA, where you would skulk around in shadowy corners looking for terrorist plots—or slip secret notes inside community mailboxes. This is where you get paid to complete different jobs around town for www.fieldagent.net or www.gigwalk.com clients. The strategy of these businesses is to provide customers with workers to carry out simple chores in their neighborhood, like taking pictures of a display in a shop. You would make money by completing activities given to you for the business.

How would you act

Field agents gather a variety of different kinds of data. You might occasionally be asked to take pictures that w will use to verify facts, document customer experiences in stores, or document how things are used. Additionally, you can be asked to do surveys and gather feedback. Fieldagent.net uses multiple-choice, multiple-select, ranking, five-star rating, freeform, and other traditional research-specific inquiry techniques. When given data assignments, field agents often combine a tried-and-true method of data gathering with modern tools like barcode scanning to guarantee the accuracy of the data. You might also be asked to gather feedback on goods or services from a Company's core customers at the Point of InfluenceTM as a field agent for one of these websites.

What to do first

The Field Agent app should be downloaded and installed as your first step if you believe you could enjoy being a field agent. The next step is to finish your field agent profile, which includes a few questions about your background. The business explicitly states that you must answer the questions truthfully to ensure that you see the appropriate employment in the system and in your location. It's probably similar to how you join up for Gigwalk.

The next step would be to click the "Find Jobs" button on the Field Agent App's main navigation window to access the "Jobs List." If you see a job (task) that piques your interest, click on it to get more information before accepting it. Once you've done that, you'll have two hours to finish the job. This means that before accepting the work, it's an excellent idea to ensure you're close to the objective (store or another retail outlet).

What do field agents make?

Jobs on Field Agent.net often pay between $3 and $12 apiece. Your Field Agent account will hold the money you earn until you wish to withdraw it, which you can do whenever your balance is more than $2. You can have the money deposited to your PayPal or Dwolla account when you pay out. There have been advertisements for things like a Hair Care Shelf Audit at $3, a Breakfast Menu Photo audit at $5, and reviewing Men's Care Special displays at $2.90 as examples of the tasks available and how much they pay.

How much money might you anticipate making?

We assume that if you could finish six assignments for $5 each, you could hypothetically make $30 each day. However, depending on what its clients need, Fieldagent.net's jobs frequently change. You can receive $30 in the first few days and then go several weeks without finding another employment in your neighborhood. Therefore, it is improbable that this would ever become a full-time job. However, you could make a fair deal of extra money working from home and on your schedule if you combined it with other jobs like CashCrate.com or interview transcription.

Perform odd jobs

Can you rewire a room, make cabinetry, paint houses, do simple plumbing repairs, and do landscaping? If so, you should search Craigslist, Task Rabbit, or https://www.taskrabbit.com/. An on-demand errand-running service called Task Rabbit combines workers with odd jobs like assembling furniture, picking up and delivering dry cleaning, and conducting online research.

Craigslist advertisements for web designers, photographers, piano tuners, architects, tax experts, bookkeepers, and math teachers are standard where we reside.

- Moving out cleaning • Window cleaning • Flooring installation
- Tailoring and changes • Product design and development • Construction accounting • Carpet cleaning
- Notary services; massage therapy; private transportation service; garage door repair and replacement
- The installation of roofing

For both Task Rabbit and Craigslist, the list is endless.

Engage in marketing

You might and should offer your services on Craigslist or Task Rabbit and update your listing regularly. Additionally, you must be willing to promote yourself rather than wait for the phone to ring. A short classified ad in your local newspaper, flyers outlining your services, and possibly hiring a teen to hand them out are some ways to do this. Be careful to inform relatives and family that you are seeking odd jobs.

Don't forget about the real estate agents in your community since they frequently know people selling their homes and need preparation work done. Members of your church or any social organization you belong to.

How much money can you anticipate making?

Another one of those topics without a clear-cut solution is this one. This will depend on how much work you want to complete in a given week and how much you can charge. This is a rough guide, but we've only engaged one handyman, whose daily rate is a fixed $200. Given his work's caliber and attention to detail, we believe that works out to $25 per hour. He can also pretty much do everything. You should be able to charge at least $40 per hour for work that needs considerable abilities, such as constructing a spa or providing electrical services. Once more, you would be your employer and be in charge of setting your hours.

You can get paid just for voicing your ideas.

You presumably have opinions on a wide range of subjects. Someone wise once said everyone has an opinion, just like everyone has a nose. But did you realize that sharing yours might earn you money? Even though you won't become a millionaire. As a result, you may still make additional money, which would only take a short while. There are three websites collecting user feedback. They are Vindale Research, Opinion Outpost, and Swagbucks. This is how they operate and what you might make. Swagbucks

You can earn money from this website by watching movies, shopping online, answering surveys, visiting your favorite stores, and more. You can even get gift cards. It has granted its members more than $100M in total. Joining Swagbucks is free, and once you're a member, you must conduct regular online activities like exploring the web, responding to surveys, watching videos, playing games, and shopping. Doing this will earn points that you may exchange for gift cards of your choice. You will also participate in daily polls, complete special offers, and ask others to join.

Opinion Source

Compared to Swagbucks, Opinion Outpost is more targeted because it pays out cash and other incentives for completing online surveys. It functions similarly to Swagbucks in that when you complete its surveys; you get points that may redeem for money or gift cards to well-known retailers. You may sign up for Opinion Outpost for free. If you do, you might start receiving payments for completing surveys about everything from politics to sports to advertisements to appliances and even what you consumed at breakfast. You are compensated for doing this because businesses value your input and will compensate you for giving it. You have two options for joining Opinion Outpost: email or sign up on its website. It differs from other survey firms in that it provides a quarterly prize draw with a potential prize pool of up to $10,000.

Vindale Analysis

For completing online surveys, this Company will pay you in cash. You receive a $2 incentive simply for signing up, and you continue to receive payments for each survey you complete. Your potential earnings would depend on the survey. For instance, it once offered a $25 survey on the healthcare and pharmaceutical industries on its website. The poll on beverage preferences earned $5.60, and the surveys on cable TV and cell phone usage paid $1.35 each. You can earn money by referring people to Vindale, and there is also a section called Daily Deals where you may earn even more money.

13. Create Articles And Make Money Off Of Them

Being a content creator is distinct from this. If you create material for websites, you must follow a timetable and write on themes given to you. For instance, if you were to produce articles about healthy eating to fulfill deadlines for a website devoted to this topic. On the other hand, in this case, you create original articles on subjects of your choice and submit them to websites. The only requirements are writing well and having a PayPal account to get money.

You publish articles to the website ArticleSale.com, which subsequently advertises them. When someone purchases your article, ArticleSale sends it, receives money, and then pays you. You can publish articles for many other categories on the ArticleSale website, including business and e-commerce, real estate, shopping, product reviews, and many others.

Compared to ArticleSale, Constant Content operates a little differently. It enables websites needing Content to specify their exact needs by giving instructions and establishing a budget. Or they may browse its library of more than 100,000 publications on virtually any topic to purchase pre-written pieces. Constant Content has articles with titles like "Why You Should Replace Your Sliding Glass Patio Doors with French Doors" for $57 or the best offer, "5 Tips to Balance Work and Family" for $27, "Five Life Habits of a Personal Assistant" for $27, and "Will Green Fuel Replace Fossil Fuel in Time to Save the Planet?" for $90 listed as examples of this.

You must be able to produce high-caliber Content if you want to write for Constant Contact. You must submit essays that have openings and conclusions.

A good amount of information Your writing must be devoid of

faults in grammar, punctuation, and sentence structure. If they pass this test, you will be compensated when others buy them because they will be listed on the Constant Contact website.
What kind of money-making writing would you do?

If you're an excellent and quick writer, this job could become a full-time one. Once you gain a reputation for producing high-quality, original Content, you might make up to $500 per week or $2000 per month if you could crank out ten articles per day or 50 per week and half of them sold.

Naturally, both websites are a little bit of a craps game. Even if you publish ten well-written pieces, you can discover a month later that not a single one has sold. However, you may earn money writing for either of these sites if you have a penchant for originality and can produce articles with catchy titles.

14. Do Drop Shipping?

You won't ever need to perform any packing or shipping, making this an excellent and straightforward method to earn additional money. However, you will need to create your own website to manage any consistent volume of transactions. This is how it goes. You decide which goods to mark up and sell on online marketplaces like eBay. Here's an illustration: A computer mouse that the drop shipper sells for $10 is listed on eBay for $15. When it sells, you send the drop shipper $10 and the buyer's details and pocket $5 for yourself. The drop shipper subsequently ships the mouse to your customer. You could list 10 or 20 of those mice figuratively and get up to $100 despite doing nothing. Listing products on eBay these days is so simple that you could potentially list 20 items in under an hour.

A list of trusted dropshipping suppliers is accessible on the Watchmen Advisors website. Using children's toys, jewelry, electronics, sporting goods, health and fitness, home and garden, gifts and collectibles, silk plants and flowers, and automobiles, among many more categories, it offers drop shippers to illustrate this. Filling out a short form will provide you with a comprehensive list of these drop shippers. List the products for the ones that appeal to you.

Additionally, Watchmen Advisors offers training, advice, and general tips for Internet marketing to small businesses. You could speak with one of its employees to receive assistance with your drop shipping tasks. It offers free and paid marketing eCourses that can educate you on all you need to know to thrive online. One of these courses is called Revenue Automation, and it teaches you the fundamentals of automation that will enable you to build as many recurring income streams as you like.

Making money using drop shipment

According to industry experts, finding niche products with little to no competition is the most excellent way to profit from drop shipping. You ought to be knowledgeable about the goods you're attempting to promote. Let's say you enjoy taking pictures. Selling digital SLRs would be a mistake because of the extensive and intense rivalry. You may sell tripods or memory cards as an alternative.

You'll require a website.

You won't merely advertise products on eBay if you want to make money drop shipping. You will require a website for your store (website). To process your orders, you will also want a shopping cart platform. Magento, Open Cart, and Zen Cart are the best of them.

Spending cash to earn cash

Finally, be ready to invest money in advertising if you want to profit from drop shipping. You might do this through Google AdWords, banner ads on relevant websites or one of the numerous ways that can advertise things can advertise things online.

15. Market Your Photos

It wasn't that long ago when you needed a dark room and a studio to sell your photographs. Nowadays, all you need is a camera owing to digital photography. Several websites buy pictures. Naturally, the more images you sell, the better photographer you are. This may be a good passive income source. Some folks have made several hundred dollars by repeatedly selling the same photo. Your photographs are automatically yours.

How it operates

There are numerous online marketplaces where you can sell your photographs. Shutterstock, 123RF, Dreamstime, and Crestock are four of the most well-known. These websites all operate pretty similarly. You create a portfolio of your photographs by creating an account, after which you upload them. There are tools you may use to describe and keyword your photographs once you've posted them. The editors of the website then review your submissions. If they do, your pictures are placed in the website's portfolio, and you get a cut of sales. This might be anywhere from $0.25 to $120. In some circumstances, the pricing of your photos will depend on the size of the image the customer chooses to purchase. Or in this case, Customers of Shutterstock have the option to download two pictures for $29. Seven hundred fifty photographs are available for $199 per month on a professional plan, or five images for $49.

Where would you sell your photographs?

Where you sell your photographs will be one of your first and most crucial decisions. A microstock agency would be your best bet if you were a product photographer. Sites like Red Stubble and Etsy may better suit your taste if you sell fine art photographs. There are essentially infinitely many micros stock agencies. When selecting one, carefully read the fine print so you know your rights, the commissions the site pays, and its rules. But when you first start, it's usually best to work with one of the well-known, large agencies like iStockPhoto (located in Canada), Shutterstock, or Fotolia.

How much you may make

Selling photographs is similar to selling written articles. You could earn a large deal or make very little extra cash.

You might make between $100 and $1000 a month if you offer extremely outstanding, distinctive photographs of trending topics. However, you might only make a pittance. Selling your images, though, would be more gratifying in many ways than just financially if you enjoy photography.

16. Get Paid To Write Freelance

A "medieval mercenary warrior" or "freelance" (meaning that the lance is not sworn to any lord's services) was what the term freelancing initially referred to. It is frequently used today to describe someone who works for themselves and isn't necessarily dedicated to a single Company over the long run.

Freelancers or individuals who work for themselves and write or perform other tasks for various businesses are typical examples of this.
There are several websites where you might obtain a job if you like writing and are a decent writer. Upwork and Freelancer are two of the biggest.

How it operates

These websites all operate similarly. After logging in and registering, you will get a list of job openings. These often include writing for websites and blogs, financial writing, copywriting, ghostwriting, and a wide variety of other writing jobs. You will be taken to a page with a description of the work, the pay, the type of employment, the skills required, and any other pertinent information when you click on one of these advertisements. If the job appears intriguing, you should submit a bid (Upwork) or a proposal (Freelancer).

How is one paid

This also differs from one website to another. Upwork pays via PayPal or direct payment to your checking account. Freelancers use only direct deposits (wire transfers) to your bank account as payment.

How much money could you make writing freelance?

The jobs listed on these websites typically pay by project or article. Writing an article can earn you as little as $5 for a short 400-word blog post or as much as $50 for a 2,000-word piece that is quite technical. There are also frequently hourly-paid projects that can be ongoing (for several years) or last only a few months.

Your reputation, the kinds of work you may acquire, and your writing speed are just a few factors determining how much money you can make as a freelance writer. We are aware of one husband-and-wife team earning more than $120,000 annually. Another statistic revealed that around one-third of respondents (freelance writers) said they made $70 an hour or more, while 23% said they made between $50 and $70. So, after you get the hang of things, you can make some good money as a freelance writer.

17. Online Education

Are you good at programming computers? Earning cash online? Creating the ideal coffee brew? Are you adept at manufacturing pottery? Do you speak Mandarin, Spanish, or French well? Can you make apps for smartphones? You might earn extra money by teaching whatever subject you are an expert in online.

locations for teaching

Udemy, Skilfeed, and Skillshare are three particularly well-liked websites. Skillshare includes classes in pattern design, email marketing fundamentals, hand lettering, and creating motion (video) content you can sell as examples of the courses offered by these websites. Using 123D Autodesk, Outsourcing Secrets Revealed, How To Quickly Make Powerful Photographic Portraits, and Learning Adwords are just a few topics on Skillfeed. There are almost 30,000 more courses available on Udemy, including Getting Started With Excel, The Complete Web Developer Course, and PHP (computer coding) For Beginners. Hence, as you can see, you could instruct in almost any subject.

What to do first

In the case of Udemy, you must first enter the course's title before selecting "Create Course." You are then directed to a page where you may enter your name, email address, and password creation. The following step is a page that will aid in the planning, creation, and promotion of your course, after

Which you can start.

You enter the name of the class you want to teach on Skillshare, sign in or create an account, and then click "Teach." This website also provides a Teach Handbook to assist you in starting, planning, and filming your lesson.
Similar to how Skillshare operates, Skillfeed does as well. You must first enter your email address and password before clicking on "Sign Up." Next, you must establish a profile and pass a few more hoops before you can post a video.

What you may potentially make teaching online

This will rely on several variables, such as the location you select, the subject or subjects you teach, and the number of students you can draw in. These three websites all provide lessons in the form of uploaded videos. You set the price for your course(s)—prices for courses on Udemy range from $25 to over $200.

Individual courses are not for sale on Skillshare. Instead, individuals join. Its teachers receive a portion of the site's monthly earnings, which is distributed in the form of royalties.

The payment system used by Skillshare and Skillfeed is similar. Students pay a monthly subscription charge. According to how long their content is viewed, instructors are paid.

How much money can you make?

One of its best features is that online teaching is passive income once your course video is finished. Your video course is uploaded, and that is all. Theoretically, if you don't do anything else, the course might make you money after three years. The instructors who make the most money online know that posting the same videos on at least two different platforms is critical. If you do this, you may easily make several hundred dollars per month.

18. Work As A Nanny Or Another Type Of Part-Time Domestic Helper

Two working parents are increasingly the heads of families today. According to a Pew Research Center research from March 2013, two working parents are present in about 60% of two-parent households with children under 18. This indicates a rising demand for nannies or caregivers who can pick up children after school, take them to school, and keep them safe and engaged until one or both parents arrive home. If this position appeals to you, numerous websites that provide nanny positions are available. ABCnannies and Care.com. Both include nanny work. Care.com also features employment providing care for the elderly and even pets. The duties of a nanny might range from simple child care to light cleaning, errand running, and even household administration.

What is necessary to become a nanny?

You must, first and foremost, genuinely like working and caring for children. Second, you would probably need to pass a background check and, if possible, submit references. You need at least two years of professional, verifiable experience, a dependable vehicle, a valid driver's license, and evidence of auto insurance to work via ABCnannies. You must be 18 years old, a high school graduate, and possess CPR and first aid certifications.

Finding nanny gigs

There are other websites for nanny jobs besides the two previously mentioned ones. You can create a free profile on Sittercity and then search for jobs. A boutique placement firm called The Nanny Network will assist you in finding and securing employment. It details working through nanny agencies, internet nanny services, or independently locating employment. It does not, however, contain a job listing. One organization is Nannies4Hire. Your profile is made. A family will contact you for an interview if they view and like your profile. eNannySource.com and Babysitters4hire.com are two different reputable websites for locating nanny jobs. Many of them run websites as well as Facebook pages.

What sort of wages could you expect as a nanny?

The national average gross weekly compensation for a full-time live-out nanny is over $700, while the national average gross weekly salary for a full-time live-in nanny is in the mid-$600s, according to the website nannytaxprep.com. With less than a year of experience, full-time nannies typically made $500 or more gross per week.

19. Blogging For Money

Have you considered starting a blog? It may be enjoyable as well as lucrative. The owner of smartpassiveincome.com, Pat Flynn, makes $153,000 a year. Collis Ta'eed's blog Tuts Plus generates $120,000 in revenue annually. The Blonde Salad, a Company, makes $200,000 a year from its blog Noupe. Another blogger's blog, Slash Gear, generates a nice $60,000 per month in revenue.
Although you are unlikely to make this much money every year from your blog, it is feasible to expect several thousand dollars from affiliate commissions, sponsored advertisements, and Google AdWords.

The freedom to select your topic is one of the best aspects of blogging. You may decide when to post to your blog, which products to highlight, and the kinds of advertisements you show. What ideas do you have for blog posts? For example, parental advice, food, sports, video games, fashion, or marketing. There are so many possibilities.
Spoiler alert: selecting a subject you are enthusiastic about is ideal. Successful bloggers publish content virtually daily. Stop for a moment and consider this. That works out to seven posts each week, 28 posts per month, and a little over 350 posts yearly. Could you imagine penning 350 pieces on a subject you don't find particularly interesting? Focus on a subject that inspires you because we think that would not be easy.

Make some inquiries

It might pay to study before getting started if you believe blogging might be your thing. You might start by searching Google with your blog's topic as your keyword. That would quickly make it clear who your rivals are. Do some reading next. Several excellent books on blogging could aid you in getting started as well as avoiding blunders. For instance, some of the best-selling books on blogs and blogging include How To Blog For Profit Without Selling Your Soul, How To Start A Blog That People Will Read, and the intriguingly titled A Work In Progress: A Memoir on Amazon. Alternatively, you could look for these books at your neighborhood library.

Do not anticipate quick results.

Trust us when we say that the bloggers that earn $100,000 or more a year didn't start at this level. They might have needed many years to accumulate this level of wealth. You'll need to exercise patience and not count on quick success. You might also need to make a small financial commitment by purchasing advertisements from Google or Facebook to get started. Getting readers is the most complex problem for any blogger. While doing this naturally (without any advertising) is possible, it is more complex and time-consuming. It will take time to build up enough traffic to start making money from your site, regardless of whether you decide to purchase advertising or go for purely organic visitors.

20. Become A Marketer For Affiliates

Becoming an affiliate marketer is a fantastic way to make money online. This entails endorsing the goods and services of other businesses in exchange for a commission. It's beautiful since you never have to store, pack, or ship anything. All of this is handled for you by the organization where you are an affiliate. You can advertise these goods on Twitter, Facebook, and other social networking sites, as well as through your blog, an online store, your articles, and pretty much any other platform you can think of.

What it does

The operation of affiliate marketing is relatively straightforward. When you register with a Company or Company, you are given unique links that you can use in your advertisements, blogs, or other content. This link notifies the business that you are responsible for the transaction when someone purchases a product you have pushed, and you are paid a commission. One of the secrets to success in this field is to advertise products that offer the best commissions, ranging from 4% to 50%. The second element is to select well-known and renowned businesses and goods so that they come with credibility. Even while Clickbank (more on this later) offers commissions of up to 50%, much fewer people are aware of it than, for example, Amazon or Wal-Mart. Simply put, selling something through Clickbank would require more time and effort than selling it through Amazon.com.

These are the top affiliate networks.

Several affiliate networks are accessible, including a few that act as aggregators or enable the sale of goods from numerous businesses. These networks are listed in order of popularity:

Amazon Unless you started selling a lot, you would only get a 4% commission. Using this affiliate network, you might market clothing, video games, audiobooks, culinary tools, or even vehicle components.
Linkshare was the last name of Rakuten (www.rakuten.com). It is one of the aggregators we previously mentioned because it allows you to advertise the goods of hundreds of different businesses, such as Starbucks, Wal-Mart, and iTunes. Although the number of Wal-Mart products you may promote must be in the thousands, we have no idea.

The website we previously stated, Clickbank (www.clickbank.com), is where you can find those generous, enticing commissions. This is because it offers information items for sale, such as cookbooks, manuals for changing how you age, and directions for using workout equipment. Its primary offering for many years was knowledge on making money online, but it has now diversified to include a wide range of information. Another fantastic benefit is that Clickbank will offer guidance on the high-demand products you could market online.

JVZoo (https://www.jvzoo.com) offers products for sale that are informational about earning money online. For instance, WP Fan Machine - Unlimited, CopyBuilder, Long Tail Pro 3.0, and Onesoci Platinum were some of its most well-liked prior products. While promoting these products to Internet marketers occupies a more specialized market than, say, selling Wal-Mart products, it is still possible to make money.

Similar to Rakuten, Shareasale is a different aggregator (https://www.shareasale.com/). It provides the chance to advertise the goods of more than 3000 different businesses. Many are more minor, specialty-oriented businesses like BuildDirect, One Kings Lane, Eco Lunchbox, and GreenKidCrafts.com. Nevertheless, there are marketplaces for all these goods; therefore, partnering with Shareasale can bring in money.
You are not required to pick only one.
The freedom from having to work with just one of these businesses is another benefit of affiliate marketing. To create the ideal store, you might collaborate with Shareasale and Rakuten and select the items you want to advertise.

21. Online Shopping Can Be Compensated For.

Do you like internet shopping? A lot of us do. What, in your opinion, would make Internet buying even more enjoyable? What about receiving payment for it? Ebates (www.ebates.com) will provide you with cash for your regular shopping. Even a bonus will be given to you simply for signing up. According to Ebates, its users have received cash back totaling more than $325 million, proving that this is no fly-by-night business. There are no forms to complete and mail in, no fees to pay, and no points to redeem in this system. The retail businesses that use Ebates pay a commission for sending customers to them, and you get cash back from these commissions. Shops like Macy's, American Eagle, Hewlett-Packard, Old Navy, Overstock, and New Balance are just a few of the merchants in Ebates. An 8% commission or double cash back used to be available from Old Navy. In comparison to Overstock, New Balance gave a 10% commission. Shopping with Dell might result in 4% cash back, and with Nike in 9%.

How it operates

When you're prepared to make a purchase, you search for the shop you wish to use and click the link to that store, creating a tracking code. You have 30 days to make purchases after visiting an Ebates-affiliated online retailer. Walmart pays Ebates 2% of each sale referred from the Ebates website as an illustration of this. So, if you use Ebates to shop at Wal-Mart and spend $500 on a computer, Ebates would profit by $10. To put it another way, Wal-Mart essentially compensates Ebates for bringing you in as a client. Ebates then divides the $10 it received from Walmart in half and provides you with $5. This results in a 1% cash rebate, a favorable bargain for all parties

Because the online stores of businesses like Wal-Mart, Best Buy, and Target benefit from the offer, this is a win-win situation. Because it receives a commission, Ebates benefits. And you, the client, benefit because you receive extra money for performing the same task you would have done anyhow.

Why is this permitted?

It's not fishy if this sounds a little off. Over 1,600 online retailers are affiliates of Ebates. In reality, practically anyone with a website can join those stores as an affiliate. If you're still unclear, consider it this way. To advertise on Ebates.com, online retailers pay Ebates. The sales commissions from these transactions were then divided between you and Ebates. It's simply another affiliate marketing type, similar to selling things on Shareasale or Rakuten.

22. Trade In Your Used Books

Many books are lying around collecting dust in most homes. So why not sell them for money? The website Bookscouter (https://bookscouter.com/) can assist you in selling them for the most money. They assess prices from many book-buying websites so you can quickly determine who will pay the most for your books. Book prices frequently change and can differ significantly amongst purchasers, so it's helpful to compare book buyers using several criteria to determine where you could sell your books at the most fantastic price.

Sell books written by others.

No problem if you don't have a ton of books of your own to sell. Books are the most specific items at the yard, garage, and estate sales. And frequently, those selling them are unaware of their true worth. Specializing in a particular genre, such as children's books, mysteries, romantic novels, or historical fiction, is one of the most excellent methods to sell books on a website like Bookscouter. When you do this, you'll understand how much books are worth and how much you should still pay for them to turn a profit. Due to people's desire to get rid of them, you can frequently discover books at yard sales and estate sales for $1 or less. Some of those $1 or $2 books might be worth $20 or more.

One of its best features is that BookScouter is free and requires no registration. However, an upgrade called BookScouter Pro costs a monthly fee. It offers you a book Lookup Tool, Bookscouter Deals, tracking, notifications, uninterrupted use, and historical vendor data if you anticipate selling many books.

Have any books?

We don't need to tell you how expensive textbooks are if you have a child in college or who has previously attended college. Selling secondhand ones on BookScouter can be a terrific option. We know one person who sells textbooks and makes $700 a month. Simply enter the ISBN of the book in BookScouter. The book can then be shipped to the reseller after you choose the best offer. Most BookScouts' resellers use PayPal or checks to make payments. Here is an illustration of what a used textbook might provide for you. N. Gregory Mankiw's "Principles of Microeconomics," seventh edition, was released in January 2014 for $271.95 on the publisher's list price. The top offer came from RentText for $91.55 when an owner uploaded its ISBN onto BookScouter in 2015. Even though it wouldn't be the same as receiving the $271.95 you paid for the book, it would still be better than receiving nothing if you just left it lying around.

Words of warning
The negative aspects of BookScouter exist. One issue is that it does not discuss resale or standards for what constitutes a book in an acceptable condition. Instead, it directs you to the reseller's website, where you must look up the permitted terms. This is crucial since you won't get paid for a book that the reseller rejects if you send it in. Another drawback is that, according to BookScouter, you shouldn't sell collectible, rare, or antique books there because you'll probably make more money selling them somewhere else.

23. Create And Market Personalized T-Shirts

Custom T-shirts are currently one of the most popular trends. The creation and sale of personalized t-shirts are effortless thanks to the website www.TeeSpring.com.

What it does

You can design a T-shirt using the online tool provided by TeeSpring. You can use fonts and clipart from TeeSpring's library or create your design. Then, you can choose the style of shirt you want to utilize or provide a variety of products, such as basic t-shirts, premium t-shirts, and hoodies. As mentioned above, you pick a sales objective, which is the minimum number of shirts you'll need to sell to have your shirts made, and you base the cost of the shirt on the profit you want to make. Any figure between 5 and 1000 is OK, and the greater your target, the more money you will earn per transaction. The TeeSpring platform will show you the expected net profits when you select a sales goal.

The next step is to select a catchy Campaign name, write a captivating title, and write a description. Your Campaign can last 3 to 21 days, but your orders won't get to your customer's homes or businesses for another 7 to 10 days.

Utilize email and social media.

Your T-shirts won't sell themselves, which is unfortunate because it would be fantastic. You must use social media and email to inform your relatives and friends about your design. You might purchase a few advertisements targeting a specific niche market. Although they will "purchase" your T-shirts, your customers won't be charged until your Campaign meets its sales target.

Generating revenue using TeeSpring

You may view the active campaigns on TeeSpring in the section titled Teeview. Visit it to find out which shirts are popular. You can sort campaigns based on sales figures or look for the most lucrative ones. Keep your design as basic as possible. Take advantage of the time of year or a current trend, if possible. This creates apparel around trends, such as famous athletic events, TV shows, or celebrities. Do not attempt to design something yourself unless you are a great designer.

Hire a designer to develop your design using Fiverr or Upwork. A variety of styles and color options are a fantastic idea so that your consumers can select the one they want. Set your sales objective low while you're first starting. Stick with a lesser quantity, such as 10 to 20, as this will work nicely and is a goal you should be able to attain if you have little to no traffic and little money for advertising.

24. List Your Expertise On Fiverr.

The services you may offer on Fiverr are very astounding. This could involve making prank phone calls, sending breakup letters, or drafting resumes. Fiverr is a terrific platform for graphic artists to sell their logos, illustrations, cartoon characters, storyboards, and avatars. If you play music, you might sell it to individuals so they can use it for their unique projects. Techies have several options to offer desktop and mobile programs and construct websites and databases.

How will you generate money if you just charge $5 per project?
One positive aspect of Fiverr is that it does away with price haggling or negotiations. You charge $5 for any service you offer.

How do you get money doing this, then?

Speed is the key to success on Fiverr. Fiverr is probably not for you if it takes four hours to make a logo. You must be able to produce between 5 and 10 gigabytes per hour. Instead of making just $5 an hour, you might make $25 to $50 an hour in this way. The traditional upsell or enhancing your services is the second method for getting money on Fiverr. For instance, you might develop a logo for $5 but charge an extra $10 or $15 if the client wants the vector file so he can edit the artwork. Additionally, you may offer the first revision free of charge but charge an additional $5 or $10 for each subsequent modification.

People who have found success on Fiverr advise choosing a service, learning it, and honing the abilities required to provide it. To promote your gig, you should be aware of your target audience and try to reach out to it as much as possible.

You must obtain a promotion.

Before being promoted to level I, where you can offer gigs for more than $5, you must first sign up for Fiverr, stay on the platform for 30 days, and complete ten orders successfully. Yes, you can sell gigs for more than $5 after that. Around 4000 services are available on Fiverr in 120 different categories, and more are being added daily. As a result of the expansion of what it refers to as its "premium" Gigs, it claims that more than 50% of these transactions are between $10 and $100. Here, experienced sellers can add to their services and charge up to $500 for them. As you may expect, these folks can achieve complete financial independence.

Last but not least, if you want to succeed on Fiverr, you must be committed, follow through on your commitments, and work extra hard to get positive customer feedback.

25. Market On Etsy

With more than 30 million users, this website has become one of the most popular on the Internet. It differs from eBay because it focuses on handmade arts and crafts, apparel, accessories, collectibles, and nostalgic objects with distinctive designs. You could sell your products on Etsy (www.Etsy.com) if you can sew, knit, crochet, carve, sculpt, work with wood, make jewelry, paint, or sketch.

Getting going

It's pretty easy to get started with Etsy. You only need to register, which you can do via your Facebook or Google account or by completing a short form. You must also supply payment information for Etsy to pay you via direct deposit. A credit card must also be on file so Etsy can charge you for your listings and transaction costs. Then simply log in and begin selling.

The price of selling on Etsy

The transaction fees on Etsy are only 3.5% of the sale, and opening an account is free. If you'd prefer not to start a store, listing an item for four months costs only $.20 U.S... Additionally, a certain percentage of your initial listings are free! If you have more than one item available, you can enable your listing to renew when an item sells automatically. Each of your listings can contain up to five images. Your listing costs, transaction fees, and the shipping labels you purchase through Etsy will all be included in a monthly payment you receive from the marketplace. The form of payment you accept, such as PayPal, is another choice. Etsy also has its credit and debit card-accepting payment mechanism called Direct Checkout. Customers can also use personal checks or money orders to make payments.

Getting paid on Etsy

You can make good money on Etsy if you like to create and make things. The same holds for antiques and collectibles, which are typically artifacts from the 1960s or before. However, it pays to conduct some market research to determine whether and how much similar products to yours are selling before you start knitting, carving, or painting like crazy. Additionally, seek for similar things to determine the best search terms. Verify the prices they are charging as well as the shipping charges. Look at the prices of the items at each end of the pricing range. This can help you determine how much to charge for your goods. Look through a few results pages to get a general sense of your rivals.

Examine which of your competitors' products are priced at the high end of the range and consider why. Similar applies to products at the low end of the pricing range.
Create an Etsy store.

You must open a shop if you plan to sell things on Etsy regularly for profit. This link will take you to pages with valuable details about naming and configuring it.

26. Market Secondhand Clothes

If you have apparel that has just seen a few wears or that you find at thrift stores, ThredUP is a terrific location to sell it. Who are we to dispute ThredUP's claim that it is the biggest online consignment shop for women's, girls', and boys' clothing?

What it does

Working with ThredUP is relatively straightforward. After registering using your Facebook or Google account, you order a Clean Out Kit. Your clothing must be defect-free, which means it must be in perfect condition without any stains, pilling, holes, or other indications of wear. Additionally, they must be "on trend" or "in season," currently fashionable. s should also use top brands like J. Crew, Mini Moden, DVF, Theory, Calvin Klein, Faded Glory, or Abercrombie.

Your Clean Out Kit will be valued by ThredUP based on its quality, quantity, and conformity to the Company's criteria when it is received. Each of your things is thoroughly inspected by ThredUP's buyers to establish its quality and viability for resale. An online earnings estimator available will demonstrate how much money other people have made by selling comparable goods.

What you'll be paid

The manufacturer's suggested retail price, the price you paid when the things were new, their age, quality, style, and how quickly similar items are selling are just a few variables that will affect how much money you can make through ThredUP—generally speaking, Will pay 10% of the item's selling price to you if the ThredUP listing price is less than $10. For apparel priced between $20 and $39.99, you'll receive 40%, and for items costing between $90 and $149.99, you'll receive 60%. There are a variety of other pricing tiers, but this should give you a general indication of how much you anticipate making on your products.

How is one paid

You will be compensated as soon as ThredUP processes any things that end up being listed for less than $60. You will be compensated when your things sell if their list price exceeds $60. When ordering your Clean Out Kit, you can choose Return Assurance if you have products that don't sell and would like to get them back.

About 50% of the clothing the firm receives is rejected, so if some of your goods are rejected, they may be donated to Teach For America, passed along to other parties for sale, or recycled into new, valuable products by the Company's textile recycling partners. ThredUP will photograph any of your products turned down so you can understand why d didn't accept them.

27. Make Money By Purchasing New Goods

Would you be interested in trying new things and getting paid for them? Through the website www.cashcrate.com, you can accomplish this. It is predicated on the idea that some businesses will pay top dollar to have customers like you test out their goods and services. Additionally, they are free to try.

signing up

It's simple to sign up with CashCrate, and doing so will earn you $1. You can get money by participating in daily research surveys, purchasing online, recommending other members to the program, and getting paid to try out goods and services.

What you may anticipate making

Two Daily Surveys, which you could do and earn $.80 for each, illustrate what you could make on CashCrate. You could make $50 per month if you completed them daily.

You can make money by seeking information on a range of goods and services when taking part in free offerings. You can view the free deals in the website's Members Area once you register. Quizzes, brief surveys, website registrations, and product trials are frequently included in these offerings. You can choose from more than a hundred offers and paid surveys on CashCrate. These will cost anywhere between $.25 to $50 for each offer.

Not every offer is free.

On CashCrate, most of the offers are gratis. There are some situations, nevertheless, where you must supply credit card details. If you are required to give this information, the reward you will receive will outweigh the cost. For instance, CashCrate might pay you $25 to try a product that costs a few dollars in shipping and handling or needs you to sign up. Despite this, you would still make a healthy profit on the transaction.

The best way to make money, according to CashCrate, is through recommendations. It claims that many of its members benefit from this and receive more than $100 monthly cheques. This process functions somewhat similarly to multi-level marketing. You will initially only receive the income you generated. However, for every referral you sign up who earns their first $10, you'll receive a $3 incentive. And this is only the start. The amount of money you make from referrals will grow as you get more and more of them.

28. Rent A Vehicle

Does your automobile spend most of the time parked or in the garage? Or do you have a spare automobile that you don't use often? So why not use it to your advantage and earn some additional cash? You can use the Turo website to rent a car from your driveway, deliver it to another place or an airport nearby, or pick it up at one of the Company's airport lots. A business called Turo, formerly RelayRides, runs a peer-to-peer carsharing marketplace. Through a mobile and internet interface, it enables private car owners to hire out their automobiles.

To begin

You may register with Turo and list your vehicle in a few minutes. To describe your car, just upload a few pictures, and presto! You're all set to move. A current calendar is required to let potential tenants know when it will be accessible. You must get your car ready before your first rental. You'll need to prepare your vehicle by cleaning the interior, keeping your maintenance up to date, and placing a RelayRides insurance card in the glove box.

According to Wikipedia, individuals can register their vehicles online to be hired by other Turo members to make money from them when they are not in use. The vehicle's owner specifies the location and time it will be accessible. A traveler who wants to rent a car makes a reservation for a specified time window online[29] and pays for the duration they select. Owners of vehicles can use Turo's dynamic pricing ideas or set their prices; the firm receives a 25% cut. The price paid by the tourists is typically 35% less than what they would pay with a conventional automobile rental firm.

Turo provides vehicles with liability insurance up to $1 million to shield owners from claims of personal injury and property damage. Except where noted, vehicles must be 2004 model year or newer and have less than 130,000 miles on the odometer. For security and trustworthiness reasons, Turo screens every user.

You have complete control.

One of Turo's most prominent features is that you have complete control over your pricing and vehicle availability. You could rent for a day, a week, or a month.
You will get requests.

When someone wants to hire your vehicle, Turo will let you know. It would help if you looked over that person's profile and reviews before deciding whether or not to rent to them. You are welcome to contact the renter if you have any questions. In other words, you decide who has permission to use your vehicle.

You will meet the tenant and verify their identification. Additionally, before giving your renter the keys, you should show them around the vehicle and check the gasoline and mileage.
When the tenant delivers your vehicle

Make careful to discuss the car's condition with the renter when you receive it back and confirm that everything is in working order. Additionally, it would help if you rated your tenant so that future landlords know what to anticipate from them.

What kind of pay should you anticipate?

Of course, how much you charge for your car will depend on whether you rent it for a day, a week, or a month. However, in

2015, the typical member made roughly $250 a month by renting out their automobile. Depending on your marketing prowess and the quality of your vehicle, you could make up to $1,000 every month.

THE SPIRITUAL IMPERATIVE: WHY YOU NEED TO START A SIDE BUSINESS

How does it look when you step back and consider your life as a whole? Imagine yourself at 80, lying in bed, reflecting on your life and all your decisions. The Greeks of antiquity "practiced death every day." To avoid being controlled by more trivial concerns, they would cultivate a broader perspective on their daily lives and enable this to permeate all of their thoughts, activities, and conduct. Meanwhile, South Koreans participate in their fake funerals to help them appreciate life more. Hospice nurse Bronnie Ware describes how many of the patients she cared for in their final days regretted that they lived a life that other people expected of them and not the life they wanted to live in her book The Top Five Regrets of the Dying. In contrast, we don't have room for regret when we use our abilities.

We are all aware of this. What is a better incentive there to pursue a career you genuinely love? When Bronnie thought her life lacked a deeper purpose, she became a palliative care specialist. While some of us look for that meaning through volunteer work or increasing our spiritual involvement, others, like Bronnie, please find a way to combine their deeper purpose with their regular jobs.

All of the clients I work with have their best moments when they decide to wager on themselves. By choosing yourself, you commit to doing the work you enjoy on your terms rather than what your boss or another authority figure expects of you. You are in a position to decide what you want to do once you leave a framework that dictates what you must accomplish. It would help if you used your free time towards this. Spend your life doing things that will nourish you.

Your decision. You are responsible for everything.
You can make far more informed decisions with a clearer understanding of your life. In his Stanford University commencement address in 2005, Steve Jobs said something that still gives me chills.

Every time I read this statement, it helps me make critical decisions in life: "Remembering that I'll be dead soon is the most important tool I've ever encountered. In the face of death, almost everything—all external expectations, all pride, all fear of failure or embarrassment—just disappears, leaving what is essential. The best technique to avoid believing you have something to lose is to keep in mind that you will die. Your undies are already on. There is no excuse not to go with your gut.

You have no choice but to start your side business if there is a difference you know you want to make in the world, and it tugs at your heart. I'm a firm believer because I've seen the incredible things that people have experienced when they take risks.

Turning your hobby or interest into a business involves switching the focus of your days from working for someone else to running your own business. Getting the life you want is the goal. That entails changing your priorities to put your needs ahead of those who are paying you. Making this shift doesn't just give you a new stream of income, which is one of its many benefits. You get a new respect for your time and effort as a result. After all, how can you grow your startup Company if you're exhausted or stressed out? This is one of the reasons starting a side business can be so reviving. It enables you to prioritize taking care of yourself over all other commitments.

Jason Wachob of mind body green believes that meditation has changed his life, which is why he practices it frequently. It supports my attention, creativity, and reduction of stress. Mary Keane-Dawson, the founder of How She Made It, stresses the importance of meditation, saying, "It's as vital to empty your mind as it is to live totally in the present, at least once a day. You restart, which enables you to review and reset your priorities regularly.

Ellie Burrows, the creator of MNDFL, is on the same page, which should come as no surprise given that her side gig was opening a meditation center. Her first piece of advice for aspiring business owners? "I would suggest that they take care of themselves before attempting to take care of a business. Humans are very tribal, and some activities require an entire village. It can be helpful to seek outside assistance, whether from a friend, life coach, therapist, or meditation instructor.

It turns out that launching a side business out of your passion—whether it be as a financial advisor, relationship coach, freelance designer, or interior decorator—is about more than just making money.

It focuses on developing your living level, maintaining your vision, creating a sense of direction, and escaping the treadmill. You affirm your value when you give your goals and abilities significant consideration. Saying "no" to those pressures that encourage you to sacrifice your quality of life to work longer hours or to accept depressing stability over empowering freedom entails doing just that. A crucial component of the jigsaw is self-care, including meditation and other activities like yoga, writing, and daily affirmations. Remember that committing to your side business means dedicating yourself to it. You must take care of Person #1! Use all the good vibes and thoughtful self-care you can muster to feed your creative side.

One of my earliest coaching clients confided in me, "Susie, all I do at work at an ad agency is study vintage jewelry and pin fashion looks together." She produced lookbooks on the weekends, followed designers on Instagram, and always wore stylish downtown attire while on a relatively tight budget. Her devotion was clear to see. She only had to take a step back to understand it. How about today, after two years? She is a personal stylist who works nights and weekends with intentions to go full-time once she has established a clientele.

What could go wrong again? She will not enjoy it. Customers will run out. She despises all of the administrative labor that goes into running a firm and will miss her former office setting (accounting, taxes, website management). Then what? She'll land a similar job to the one she just had (that might even pay more).

What is the best that could happen, then? She works at something she is completely enamored with and becomes a successful CEO. She publishes a book on fashion. Top trendsetters become her best friends, and designers follow her on Twitter. She is relocating to Paris. She works with famous people and spends the winters there. She starts selling her valuables. The future? There are countless alternatives. I live in potential," said Emily Dickinson. So does my client, I suppose. You, too, can, but only if you start.

I recently talked with a buddy who inquired about my hourly rate. It made me pause because I no longer think about this issue in my daily life. When I was working, I used to dislike coming into the office after 5 o'clock or leaving for home after a business flight and missing my husband's dinner—her amazement at my response (and me). I remarked that my calendar is usually packed, yet I never feel like I'm working. That, in my opinion, was pretty cool! It was almost as if the cosmos was telling me I was on the correct path. I was occupied yet never at work. What is superior to that?

Next to you

Write a letter to yourself when you are 80 years old. Begin by saying, "Dear Me, I'm so glad I've never been terrified. I'm so grateful that I.

Then, list everything you've always wanted to accomplish as an older version of yourself.
Here are some excellent questions to ask this older, wiser version of yourself when you begin a conversation. What do you want?

Where am I reserving myself?

What will I do to reward myself for having the fortitude to do?

What aspect of myself do I genuinely need to cherish and uphold (even if doing so goes against what others demand of me)?

What gives me a sense of joy and vitality?

How can I prioritize my pleasure and tell the truth above anything else?
Don't be reluctant. Allow everything to the surface, even if it makes you uncomfortable. This may extend beyond the influence you have through your work. But I'm confident that finding employment you love will rank high.

WHY YOU SHOULD START A SIDE BUSINESS: THE BENEFITS IN REAL LIFE

We've now discussed the motivating aspect of things. Let's now get down to business. With our short time on earth and the enormous untapped skill and creativity we know we possess, we should ideally be pretty sure that we need to sate our inner need to enrich our lives. We must take advantage of it, nourish it, and watch what develops. Not doing is unhealthy. However, there is also a practical case for doing it, as previous chapters on generating income streams should have indicated. Let's review.

Here are a few primary causes:
There is no longer such thing as the job stability. Therefore you insure against an unstable economy.
You can feel good about your daily $4 cappuccino, pay off some debt, or take that vacation because you earn more money.

You acquire new skills that are essential in this day and age, such as WordPress, sales, marketing, negotiation, networking, and customer relations management (CRM), as well as fundamental accounting and taxes principles. Skills may help you till you no longer need them in your day job.

Since I started life coaching without a website, business cards, or office, setup fees can be meager. Instead of having my own office, I charged $100 per hour, met individuals through my network (LinkedIn, Facebook), and saw clients at coffee shops or via Skype. Additionally, I persuaded my employer to pay for my coaching studies. You can find budgets you were unaware of if you ask and speak out for them!

You can fit it into your calendar; you have access to the evenings and weekends, and you have access to a vast amount of hours if you recognize that capacity is a state of mind.

You can work as a freelancer for websites like 99designs, Fiverr (I was just reading about a woman who makes $9,000 a month doing voice-overs; it was initially a side gig), Upwork, and Freelancer.com, which offer jobs ranging from website bio writing to book cover design and language translation; this makes it even harder to come up with excuses.

You have a profit! Consider this. While establishing your business, you cannot go to the bar, sample sale, four-hour lunch, or shop for ballerina flats or golf clubs online.
One day you'll be able to inform your employer you're leaving because your earnings from side jobs are equal to (or greater than) your pay.

You might create, publish, or develop the following big product that people demand.

Unlike your (presumably) constricting career, the opportunities are limitless. No salary limitations or glass ceilings here!

If you're still not convinced, keep in mind that Sara Blakely developed Spanx while working full-time as a fax machine salesperson (she didn't quit her job until Spanx became one of Oprah's favorite products). While working full-time in a hospital, Khaled Hosseini penned the bestselling book The Kite Runner. As he concluded his residency, Michael Burry continued his love of financial investment in between shifts at Stanford Hospital. Shortly after, he quit practicing medicine to focus full-time on his side business, founding a highly lucrative hedge fund and earning hundreds of millions of dollars by correctly predicting the subprime mortgage crisis. He served as the subject of Michael Lewis's book The Big Short and was portrayed by Christian Bale in the film adaptation.

You don't believe you have what it takes to be that successful, do you? Reconsider your position. Although she is unaware of it, Eat Pray Love author Elizabeth Gilbert has been a significant mentor to me. "I am 46 now, and I look back at the people who I was hanging out with in my 20s, and there were those who had what looked to me at the time like endless power and infinite promise and infinite possibility," she said in an interview with Cosmopolitan. And they never used it in any way. There were also some individuals who I kind of

I had written off and assumed I didn't have anything, but those people blew my mind with what they eventually produced; who has talent and who doesn't is the most boring question in the world. Since I've realized that's not the situation, We'll never find out. We cannot distinguish between gifted people and those who are not using any objective metric. Only what they produce and how they live their lives can reveal this. How much inherent talent I possess is unknown. I am aware that I put in more effort than anyone I know. I worked as a server, a bartender, and a bookkeeper while I was in my 20s. Work ethic and a willingness to pursue your goals are more crucial. And as you may know, I wrote my first two books while working three jobs. I, therefore, occasionally hear individuals say, "I would want to accomplish this, but I don't have time!" I often hear that people aren't devoted enough when they say, "Well, I have a real job, and I would have to quit my job to write a book."

How will you strengthen your dedication? I had brunch with two recent college graduates who work as sales directors in the online advertising industry. Both are accomplished and intelligent. One of them confided in me her concept for starting an event planning Company focused on a particular sector of the economy. The idea has immense potential. But allow me to share a little secret with you. Ideas are worthless. A decent concept carried out is preferable to a great idea just discussed over waffles and mimosas.

When she first mentioned it, she immediately began finding flaws in it, saying things like, "Well, I want to move out of New York one day so that it won't be sustainable," and "I don't have any expertise in the hospitality sector." Ah, our old friend, fear, you're back. Are you kidding me? I wanted to shout. You work in sales! You overcome all obstacles to close business in one of the cutthroat industries ever!

I know she repeatedly phoned a client to set up only one 30-minute meeting during her day job. Do you believe this young woman could not find a few locations to speak with her and present her thoughts in the same manner she does every day she works? And doesn't there always be some sort of event in every city in the nation? So I questioned her, "Well, how might it work if you believed it could?" It would help if you also asked yourself this when your doubts start to sneak in.

What abilities do you have that might be advantageous in this situation?

How might it succeed in a manner you haven't necessarily considered?

This intelligent young lady used those three inquiries to find the answer to her issue. I'm a salesperson, she realized. I am skilled at persuasion. I am adept at selling concepts. Just do your homework (dong, ding, ding!) and adjust it for a new market, please!

It's official, my friends.

She is on the path to designing her ideal life now that she has this realization. How may that appear to you? Dan Kolansky, CEO of Champions Of The Web, accomplished this using the extra money he made from creating business websites and internet advertising campaigns. He says, "It funds my love of hobbies like photography and camping and allows my wife to stay home with the kids. In the long run, I hope to achieve financial independence and be able to devote the majority of my time to my family and local community development. Ironically, my Company has already given financial independence to several clients. Time to take care of myself.

It gives you the confidence to accept responsibility for your work, money, and time. The number of people who believe their corporate abilities, or any expertise they may have from years of employment, cannot be applied to a side business amazes me. I'm here to tell you that c can also apply much of your knowledge from your job experience in beneficial ways.

Besides, you'll be better positioned to negotiate with your day job thanks to your side business. Your money is neither capped nor your horizons, says Dan. You can just tell them to pound sand and continue with your life if you don't like your employment for whatever reason. You become more beneficial to your employer as a result. The power in the relationship shifts to you if they know that your side job is providing you with an equivalent amount of money or more. You don't need them, but they do need you. This makes it very simple to request special consideration, additional time off, raises, or the like. It also gave me confidence when speaking with my supervisor (which improved our relationship)." Your life will always be better if you make progress in one area.

I'll share one of Paulo Coelho's The Alchemist's significant discoveries with you if you haven't read it already: "Everything is one," In other words, there aren't any discrete life lessons we learn or experiences we have that won't be useful to us in the future. Even the tedious aspects of our previous employment—for example, data input and revenue tracking in an Excel spreadsheet—might have taught us valuable lessons we can apply to our new businesses. Everything is connected. This can also be an excellent chance to learn new talents, which will only increase your flexibility for

Any upcoming endeavors. Have a fantastic concept for an app but are putting it off due to your coding anxiety? When you sign up for a free online tutorial, you'll have access to the tools you need to design your own digital products and gain new skills that will build out your knowledge base. Learning new programming skills increases your marketability, boosts your confidence, and frees you from being constrained by perceived impossibilities. Your new programming skills may suddenly qualify you for a promotion into a new role or department at your day job. Never accept the conclusion that "I don't know how"; if others can accomplish it, you can too!
To be ready for any changes or difficulties, part of side hustling is constantly developing yourself. If not, both your career and your

enthusiasm for life will stagnate.

What is there for you to lose? Your regular job will continue. Your rent is still being paid. Your day work still provides for you in the same manner as before. You continue to have health coverage. By starting your own business, as NatureMapr CEO Aaron explains, "you have lowered your level of risk, you don't need to dilute your firm and take external financing, and you can do it on your terms."

You are the one in charge.

Other significant tangible advantages of a side business include the following:

Own hours to be set. This is especially advantageous for parents, caregivers, and tourists. What might it look like for you to be in charge of your week, month, or year? How may this benefit not only you but also those nearby? Perhaps you would spend the afternoon working three hours while your kid napped or attended part-time daycare.

The chance to use extra money to reduce debt or save for a specific goal. What might you and your family accomplish with an additional $500, $1,000, or $5,000 each month?

You are gaining new abilities and improving your desirability in future job searches. A fantastic method to explore a new career by dipping your toes in the water of a different industry is to have a side business. Once you're making enough money and are ready to make the big move, it may also give you the confidence to quit a lousy boss.

They are establishing protection against job loss or layoffs. What chances and flexibility would your improved cash flow and business skills give you if things go south this year, next year, or in five years?

Unfortunately, Homeland repeats won't help you achieve your long-term objectives. It would help if you got to work. Therefore, let's begin. Commit to generating additional revenue, and set financial targets and objectives to create accountability. That requires delving into specifics! When will your first client come in? What costs would your side business help you with? As you grow your new Company, setting specific financial benchmarks will assist in keeping your focus on the goal. Make a schedule and monitor your progress for each milestone you want to hit. Are you on my side?

Next to you

Considering your hustle idea once again, ask yourself these questions:

Can I dedicate how many hours a week to growing this business?

What network can I tap into, or who can I contact to get influence for my next move?

What amount must I pay each month to replace my lost benefits and current salary?

What abilities do I have that might be useful in this situation?

How might it be successful in a way I haven't necessarily considered?

CONCLUSION: THERE ARE COUNTLESS POSSIBILITIES.

"Man frequently becomes what he thinks he is. It's possible that if I keep telling myself that I can't do something, I'll be unable to do it"

Mahatma Gandhi

"Without imaginative leaps or daydreaming, we lose the thrill of potential. After all, planning is a type of dreaming"

Glory Steinem

Here's a little-known fact that applies to everyone. The universe meets you halfway when you move toward your goals, take the initiative, get busy, and gather momentum. Steven Pressfield refers to this as "help" in his book Do the Work. It is genuine. No matter what name it goes by—positive thinking, the law of attraction, or something else—the advantages are still there. This emphasizes how important it is for everyone to have a positive outlook on our situation without downplaying the actual issues we all encounter in life.

I'll give you some examples of how help has come to me in the past—not just once, but several times—to inspire you to stay committed to your own goals. Being open enough to see it is the key! I was a little bored and uneasy at work in June 2012, but I hadn't yet started side hustling. I had no idea that you could go it alone, and I had no idea where to start or what I would do. I was concerned that my supervisor would become upset if I did not devote all my attention to selling advertising technology. (You'll be relieved to learn that this is becoming less and less true. Government employers are the main exception, but many encourage creative endeavors outside the workplace unless severe contractual obligations bind you.)

A co-founder of the startup I was working for unexpectedly called me for a job opportunity. To test if I might make any money from political advertising, he asked if I would be interested in working in Washington, D.C., for the rest of the year. I have no idea why he asked me, but I like to imagine that he did so because he thought I was someone who got things done and was open to trying new things.
I have never done anything like this before. Being a Briton by birth, I have no idea what the American political system is like. Nada. Zip. Zero. I didn't even know who Obama's Republican opponent was at that moment; all I knew was that he was running again. To fill in the gaps in my knowledge, I not only gave myself a crash course in American politics but also binge-watched CNN and devoured Politico.

Then, from June through November, I spent most of my time in Washington, D.C., pitching political action organizations and advertising firms on video Campaign ideas. Political Sales Director was my new title, and the W Hotel across from the White House became my second home. In Washington, DC, the cabbies knew me. I was surprised he knew my destination as I hurried into his car on my phone with my high heels and a small suitcase. "Back to the W?" he inquired.

I gave that particular, challenging, and intricate market my all as if my life depended on it. One evening, I even had two steak meals back-to-back at 6:30 and 9 o'clock to accommodate two different client schedules.

My manager claimed he would have been "thrilled" if I had brought in $500K in advertising revenue. By the time the final West Coast voting polls closed on November 3, 2012, I had amassed approximately $3 million. What lesson does this tale teach us? Should I establish myself as a political expert? No. Had I discovered my niche in Washington? Not. The lesson here is that you don't have to conform to whatever stereotypes people have of you to do great things.

I had zero political experience. I wasn't even eligible to vote because I wasn't a citizen of the United States. I had never sold media campaigns before. I didn't have any motivation to be successful other than my unwavering work ethic and belief that I could. Why not me, as Mindy Kaling is fond of saying?

Making that experience great (and receiving a delicious little bonus as a result—another lesson learned, always ask for more) demonstrated what can be accomplished quickly with a lot of effort and conviction. What's more? The largest contract I closed, worth over $800K, resulted from a random tip from a recent acquaintance.

On my way back to New York, I had a last-minute meeting with a little firm that I had never heard of before, and I almost couldn't make it work. But I had a calling to leave. This was not a meeting I had worked so hard to set up. It was a slight worldwide wink and benediction, commending my effort and commitment. When you become busy, the universe meets you halfway and over-delivers —always unpredictable but more intense than you can imagine. I have heard countless tales similar to this. This I am sure of. We too frequently deny the cosmos the chance.

We either start too late or don't even try.

When f finalized this significant agreement, my boss purchased champagne for the entire New York office and sent an email to the entire business with a picture of me opening the bottle. It was pretty fantastic, man. I had a rock star feeling. At the holiday dinner for the entire international team in San Francisco that year, I was presented with one of the five corporate awards. Ironically, I was with my spouse in Turks & Caicos and could not comprehend it. I had the impression of being one of those fantastic dudes who couldn't accept their VMA because they were on set or doing something cool abroad. Hey, what the heck? A girl can dream.

Another time my husband Heath and I truly needed it, the cosmos rocked for us. We live in the United States because of our health. His dedication brought us to New York after his employer moved him here at 23, and he successfully negotiated (and obtained) green cards for us. Anyone who has gone through the green card application process knows how laborious and drawn-out it is.

More than anywhere else, we adore living in the United States. So Heath obtained us green cards through his Company with significant help from the general public. After spending seven years in one organization, he was prepared to locate a new position better suited to his long-term ambitions. He had put in a lot of effort for us over the years, so starting a job search in such a cutthroat market felt overwhelming. Also, it's normal to feel a little nervous about switching to work for a large American corporation after spending seven years with an Australian Company and work culture. However, the universe came through once more.

I was in Miami on a professional trip. Many factors are at play here, so you simply have to trust the universe! The trip was delayed twice due to my client's schedule, and we ultimately stayed at the Viceroy Hotel after almost choosing another hotel. Heath decided to remain the weekend with me.

Since I was ready before him and we had decided to eat dinner in the hotel, I went to the bar to get a martini. Just as the man next to me had his lunch, which appeared to be exquisite, I sat down. We started discussing the menu after I inquired about what he had ordered. When Heath came, we had the typical small talk with strangers about things to do in Miami and our origins. The man was a managing director and business head at a Company that Heath truly wanted to work for. Due to that chance encounter, he was recruited two weeks later. A slam dunk!

Consider how everything worked together to provide my husband with this opportunity: the date, the hotel, the timing at the bar, and the open seat. Luck? I don't believe it.

So. Invariably, something more than we can see or comprehend is at work.

Here is my last example of how the universe is on your side. My employment ended in December 2014. It was a big and frightening decision, but I was exhausted after over 18 months of side hustling (and an average of $4,000 a month doing it). With my supervisor, I didn't have a smooth rhythm. We had recently moved into a new apartment, and I knew I would be safe if I decided to work full-time in this new environment. Although it was horrifying, I also felt I had no other option. This was my opportunity to put my faith into action, live out what I preach, and take a gamble. After all, I used to ask myself, "Hey, what if it does work out?" whenever I needed a lift.

Going full-time in my hustle was quite challenging the first month. Heath left the House every morning shortly after six in the winter. I was by myself and felt incredibly egotistical and guilty. Although it wasn't easy to leave a corporate position after more than ten years, I kept myself busy writing and scheduling new clients. I had no acquaintances who were also business owners. Everyone else spent the whole day at work.

What exactly was I doing? It seems foolish, but when I glanced at my closet full of jackets and heels, I felt I had lost the need for the accessories that gave me a sense of importance. I experienced fear, uncertainty, and a great deal of self-doubt. Had I acted appropriately? I forfeited a substantial income in a flourishing sector. One of the priciest cities in the world was where I resided. Having come from such a low-income home, some of me struggled to accept my behavior. Was I a fool?

I took a plane to the U.K. to see my mum, and I returned afraid and depressed. Although significant change is challenging, it should have been an exciting period. There's no way to sugarcoat it.
It did so for almost a month. I updated my LinkedIn profile as usual and replied to recruiters, informing them that I wasn't interested in full-time jobs (feeling unsure and heavy as I did). I then had a thought. I questioned whether anyone would consider using me as a consultant, adviser, or coach to help them grow their businesses.
I could bundle my life coaching, sales, and general business knowledge to provide senior management at high-growth Silicon Valley firms with advice. (Consultants are familiar with D.C., and I know what they do and how they operate.)

I met the first two persons with whom I discussed this concept over coffee. They both desired to retain my services as a business advisor. My good fortune was unbelievable! Godspeed, Universe.

I'm not sharing these tales with you to boast. I'm telling you this because I want you to know that if we continue to be proactive, receptive, and open, we have more beautiful chances than we currently perceive. Despite your introversion—

Remember that you live in the most significant era because the Internet is your best buddy. From the comfort of your sofa, you may communicate with anyone, anytime, anywhere, without ever leaving your current location or opening your mouth. I have "friends" in international business Facebook groups that I am now doing business with but who I will probably never meet in person or even speak to on Skype.
Examine your assumptions about your capabilities. It doesn't take much to tweet an influencer you like or to leave a remark on an Instagram snap. These people will get to know you over time! So don't worry! Social media is simply that; you never know where it can take you. Consider your personality while choosing an approach, and don't assume there aren't any other possibilities.

Protect your thoughts like a bulldog when you're uncertain. Rely on the reasons why something WILL work out when doubts appear. I still have a list of reasons why everything will go right for me on my phone at any point in my life. They consist of clients who will always use me as a fallback, a reminder of the extent of my unique online network, and my devoted husband and close friends.
Since childhood, my mother and I have been fascinated with self-help books, searching secondhand bookstores for high-quality titles at reasonable prices. I currently write self-help books.

Are you so limited by time? Begin anyhow. Unsure of your area of passion? Begin anyhow. Self-doubting? Begin anyhow. I have you. What if everything does work out? Consider this scenario while putting all doubt, worry, and anxiety aside.

Then fasten your seatbelt. Breathe in deeply.
And be ready for it to materialize.

Why Do I Want to Hustle?
Want to discover the reason?

It's not for financial gain. It's not to run a Company as its CEO. It's not to exercise complete creative control or to deliver that long-overdue letter of resignation. It's necessary because you are capable, because you matter, and your contribution matters.

Yes, I can provide you with advice, shortcuts, and tactics that will hopefully reduce your frustration level, let you know you're not traveling alone, and make your long evenings spent in front of your computer, studio, or workshop a bit more bearable. But what is more crucial than the framework, the guidance, and the experience of others? All gathered here? Inner knowledge. The knowledge that inspires you to produce something. That whisper encourages you to move onward, the one that persists even when you're feeling depressed. The voice was telling you to move forward.

Respect that insight. It is legitimate. Hey, what if it does work out? It prompts you to think.

Let's find out then.

www.ingramcontent.com/pod-product-compliance
Lightning Source LLC
Chambersburg PA
CBHW050331220526
45465CB00018B/1309